WORDS ON HIGH

Poetry and Inspired Events from MAB

MARC A. BEAUSEJOUR

WESTBOW
PRESS
A DIVISION OF THOMAS NELSON

WestBow Press books may be ordered through booksellers or by contacting:

WestBow Press
A Division of Thomas Nelson
1663 Liberty Drive
Bloomington, IN 47403
www.westbowpress.com
1-(866) 928-1240

ISBN: 978-1-4497-1494-9 (e)
ISBN: 978-1-4497-1495-6 (sc)
ISBN: 978-1-4497-1496-3 (hc)

Library of Congress Control Number: 2011926102

Printed in the United States of America

WestBow Press rev. date: 4/13/2011

ACKNOWLEDGEMENTS

First of all, I would like to thank my Lord and Savior Jesus Christ for allowing me to serve Him this way and serve others as well. It wouldn't be possible without Him. I would like to thank my family and my parents, Jean and Lineda Beausejour for raising me and even though I may have been unbearable at times, you never gave up on me. Even though times are hard now, you are a living proof that God will always make a way. I would like to thank the people I grew up with in Richmond Hill and the brothers and sisters in Bethany French Baptist Church in Jamaica, New York led by Pastor Pierre Leonidas and Pastor Eddy Bichotte for inspiring the events in my life. I also thank the Good Samaritan Haitian Alliance Churches in Kennesaw and Lawrenceville for your continued prayers and positive influence in the ministry. I thank Eastwood Baptist Church and the American congregation for taking us in giving us a home and developing me in ministry. I extend my deep gratitude to Westbow Press for your consideration and your assistance in making this dream a reality for me. May God continue to bless you all and may the words in this book touch your hearts.

MAB

CONTENTS

DEDICATION

I would like to dedicate this book to a special friend, Melinda Petty. It has been four years since the Lord took her home, but I know that she is walking the streets of gold and spending every day in the presence of God. All I have to say is, "You knew." You knew how much potential I had to write a book of poetry, and you believed in me, even though I did not believe in myself. Thank you for your faith in me. I wish you were here to see me now, but just as it was in God's divine plan for us to meet when I was only fourteen, it was God's plan for you to meet Him face-to-face. I'm glad the suffering is over for you. I thank God for your family, because all of them have been a big influence in my life.

INTRODUCTION

Many of you are probably wondering why I am writing a book so early in my life. I mean, I'm only twenty-two, I'm still working on a bachelor's degree, and I have my whole life ahead of me. At this time I'm supposed to be out enjoying every weekend, focusing on school, and doing something meaningful for my life. But the thing about it is that this *is* my life. I love to write, I love to share my experiences with people, and I enjoy influencing other people's lives through my works.

This is not just a book of poetry. This book also contains the inspiration and the moments that led me to write my poems. My life revolves around love for God, my family, and my ambition to succeed—but my life also revolves around poetry. If you told me about twelve years ago that I was going to write a book that contained most of the poems I've written throughout the years, I would have looked at you like were crazy. Me? Marc A. Beausejour, the tall, awkward, lanky kid with the unusually long last name who is virtually scared shy of everyone he comes in contact with? No, not me. But I was always told as a little boy in my Christian upbringing that God had a plan for my life. It may not be what I want or see, but God is the potter; I was just His clay. I had to step aside and let Him mold me into His image. He wanted me to write my poems so they would inspire, instruct, and entertain His people.

At first I was reluctant, because I wanted to shape my future my way—at my own time. Even though I was quiet as a boy, I still struggled with pride. Growing up in Queens, New York and Kennesaw, Georgia, I felt like I had to walk around with my chest puffed out like a peacock, strutting around like I was one of Hollywood's A-list actors. But Jesus said in Matthew 5:5, "Blessed are the meek, for they will inherit the Earth." Being meek is described as being powerful, but humble—not showboating, displaying yourself, or drawing any type of attention to yourself, like I see so many people try to do today. The secret to being meek isn't *forcing* people to see your greatness, but *allowing* people to see your greatness. Let your works manifest themselves, and people will see your true potential.

I've had a lot of great leaders and instructors throughout my life who have displayed meekness proficiently and efficiently. Throughout this book, I will mention those leaders. All my gratitude, affection, and blessings go out to them. If I forget to mention a couple of people, I want to apologize beforehand, for you are all influential in my life. I will also mention some people I remember growing up with, my memories as a child, and how my experiences shaped me into the person I am today.

This book is by no means a novel of any sort; it is just a testimony of my early upbringing, my background, and many adventures described through poetry. I've been writing poems ever since the seventh grade, but I have loved writing for as long as I can remember. One of my earliest memories of writing was when I was seven years old and living in Queens, New York. I had just gotten into trouble with my mother, and I was told to wait till my father got home. *Uh-oh!* When I got in trouble with my mother, she usually just spoke to me—unless she was *really* mad; then I would get a spanking or something for me to remember so I wouldn't misbehave again. But back then, I thought my father was ruthless. *Ruthless.* To me, there was just no speaking to him when he got mad, so I awaited my fate. Then out of nowhere, as if a sign from God himself, I had an idea. If I could show my father how deeply sorry I was for misbehaving and that I was sincere, maybe I could avoid the belt. In haste, I quickly wrote a letter to my father, apologizing to him. I used many sophisticated words to earn brownie points (well, sophisticated for a seven-year-old) and I put the letter on the counter shelf where I knew he would see it when he came home.

Sure enough, he came home and saw the letter. When he read it, he called me and said, "Marc did you write this?" I nervously nodded my head yes, my knees still knocking together, sweat beads starting to form. In the past I would always know when I was about to get a spanking from my father—when his face glared slowly, as if in slow motion. I knew that if he developed a glare while reading the letter, it was all over. As he finished reading the letter, I never saw the glare come to his face. But he did inform me that what I did was wrong and to never do it again. *Yes!* It looked like I was in the clear. At that time, I realized that the letter probably saved me a spanking.

Ever since that moment, I loved to write. I would write journals, stories, comics, and plays throughout the course of my childhood. Poetry wouldn't come until later on, but I knew that writing was something I had to stick with. This may be one of the funniest or most pointless stories that you've ever read, but it complies with what I aim to do with this book. I'm hoping that my writing changes people's views—the way they take life—and help and encourage them to use whatever gift they have for God. Nothing makes me more discouraged than to see people who have gifts and abilities that God has blessed them with but don't use those gifts for God—or they use them for the wrong reasons.

Music was essential in my life when I was growing up. I grew up with my homeland music—*zouk* and *kompa*—blaring in all the radios. As a kid, I most often listened to Christian music; my parents did not want to expose me to any worldly music. However, in the neighborhood I was living in, I *was* exposed to the music, and I remembered listening to artists such as Biggie Smalls, Tupac Shakur, Nas, Wyclef Jean, and the late, great King of Pop, Michael Jackson. All of these people were talented artists, and they were good at the music they sing and the people they inspire with some motivational hits. But as gifted as these artists were, did they use their talents to glorify God? It wasn't until late in my teen years that I learned that I couldn't listen to their music and still call myself a child of God. I thought of how much greater these artists would have been if they used their God-given gifts to praise God. I decided that if I was ever going to enter the entertainment industry, I was going to use my gifts solely for the purpose of the Lord Jesus Christ and the kingdom of heaven.

As you will see, my poems involve real-life issues and situations. For example, the first poem that I have in this book is titled "Kinbe Ayiti nan men ou", which means "hold Haiti in your hands" in my native language, Creole. Other poems contain bits and pieces of my life, and some describe the people that I have associated with. This book is also equipped with scriptures from the NIV (New International Version) Bible that will further explain the deeper meaning behind the poems that are written. All in all, this will make for very good reading during your break at work, while you drink coffee at breakfast time, or when you settle in for the night. So sit back, relax, and let your mind delve into my eyes and my thoughts through my poems.

PART 1

The History and the Beginning of My Inspiration

"In the beginning you laid the foundations of the earth,
and the heavens are the work of your hands"
(Psalm 102:25) (NIV).

CHAPTER 1

The Motherland: Haiti—The History of Haiti

Kinbe Ayiti nan men ou

A local kid talks and plays as the palm trees sway,
before the 103-degree day forces him to the beach where adults lay
The child has no shoes. but it wasn't considered a concern
He only seeks shade to avoid being sticky and sunburned
Then the sun sets; dinnertime looms, and he can smell the spice
The aroma is nice; a mixture of *jurie a' poi,* beans, and rice.
But before he eats, he bows his head in humble reverence
to give thanks for the fine food which he considers a decadence
Because there is evidence that God still provides in abundance
In the prayer, the boy says, "God, no matter what we go through
No matter what we see or what we do, *kinbe Ayiti nan men ou.*"
Here in our motherland, we aren't looking for remorse or pity donation
We are looking for a miracle healing in our small nation.
We are people like any other, trying to make a decent living
But due to tyranny that surrounds us, life hasn't been forgiving
For some families the threats of kidnappings and ransoms fill the air
And yet there is a whole wide world that doesn't seem to care.
Our country is viewed as a disaster, our norms and values a tragedy
Everyone else considers us the third world's biggest fatality
But if you know the heart of a Haitian, this doesn't always ring true
Which is why we must ask God, *kinbe Ayiti nan men ou.*
So whether people know me by acquaintance or by name,
I, for one, am proud to have Haitian blood run through my veins.

"*L'union fait la force.*" These are the quotes that are written at the bottom of Haiti's national flag. "There is strength in unity." It's easy to say those words from our mouths, but how many of us believe that we are able to put our differences aside and unite to become a strong nation?

Located in the heart of the Caribbean, Haiti has a land mass of 10,714 square miles. The word *Haiti* is an Indian word, meaning "mountains," which suits the island, because most of Haiti's landscape is made up of mountains. Only 20 percent of the territory lies below 600 feet. I think it's safe to say that it never gets cold there, because the average temperatures there range from 80 to 86 degrees from January to July. The summers are sweltering, and most of the residents are outside frequently—going to market, going to the beach, or just relaxing. The mountain's view is beautiful and scenic, and it is great for tourists passing by who want to take pictures to take a piece of the history home with them.

Haiti is part of an island shared with Dominican Republic called Hispaniola. Back in 1492, Christopher Columbus landed on Hispaniola and claimed it for Spain. The Spaniards actually built the New World's first settlement at La Navidad on Haiti's north coast. Around 1697, the Treaty of Ryswick divided the island through St. Domingue. For over one hundred years, the French controlled the west side of Hispaniola, enslaving about five hundred thousand people—most of western African origin.

In 1791, the rebellious slaves had enough and revolted against the French colony led by Toussaint L'ouverture and officers Jean-Jacques Dessalines and Henri Christophe. They fought to gain Haiti its independence.

In 1804, Haiti finally won its independence from France. It became the second republic in the Western Hemisphere since the United States gained independence from Great Britain. The Haitian flag colors of blue and red were created by turning the colors over and removing the white band; these were France's flag colors. Talk about putting salt on the wound! After Haiti gained its independence, there would still be rebellions and betrayals that would plague the country for about twenty more years before Jean Pierre Boyer became president of the republic in 1820.

Haiti was once a peaceful, beautiful, prosperous island on which people could take vacations, go to resorts, and relax. But political unrest and government tyranny continued to plague this little island. After Dr. Francois Duvalier, who was president of Haiti from 1964 to 1971, died in office, he was succeeded by his son, Jean-Claude (Baby-Doc) Duvalier. Jean-Claude Duvalier's term as president would see sickness, endless massacres, and a large amount of people packing up their bags to eagerly leave the tyrannical government. In 1986, protests against "Baby Doc" lead the US to arrange for Duvalier and his family to be exiled to Spain. President Prosper Avril then took over the presidency from the late 1980s to 1990, where Jean-Bertrand Aristide (who was a parish priest) took over as president in a democratic election. But by then, Haiti was merely a shell of what it used to be. The country still had civil unrest—and even worse, there was widespread use of voodoo. Even though Roman Catholicism was the most widely practiced religion, voodoo was considered the national religion.

There are so many rites and rituals involved in the practice of voodoo that explaining them would probably take up 75 percent of this book. Voodoo does involve good and evil spirits that possess children and adults alike, and there are ritual dances that must be performed. My father has told me stories, and I've seen footage of unaware, unknowing children who bathed in what looked like blood and did many other sacrificial actions to commune with those spirits.

I've heard from many churches that the reason Haiti is suffering economically and politically is because of the island's dedication to the practice of voodoo. Honestly, I don't know how to feel about those statements. Half of my inner being agrees, because if you read the Bible, there were times that the people of Israel turned from worshipping God and started to serve Baal, the god of Canaan. What happened afterwards was described—sicknesses, crops that were not fertile, neighboring countries that would invade—it was a string of one bad event after another. Another part of me, however, does not attribute the country's struggle primarily to the practice of voodoo. There are other factors, such as income, government, and lack of supplies needed to improve housing and living conditions. But as the poem explains, God will always hold Haiti in His hands. Just when we are about to give up on life altogether and things seem bleak, God keeps His people united.

On January 12, 2010, Haiti suffered its worst blow yet when a 7.0 earthquake shook Haiti, killing thousands and leaving others homeless. I was actually at my job when I first heard about the earthquake. I had just clocked out at my usual time, and I received a call from my brother, Jonathan. He said that an earthquake had just struck Haiti at around 5:00 p.m. I was just stunned. I experienced mixed feelings, and it wasn't until I arrived home that I realized my aunt was in Haiti. My uncles were in Haiti. My *entire extended family* was in Haiti. I remember the house being eerily quiet, with the only being the CNN reporter who was describing the disaster. I instantly prayed to God, "Please, God, just see if my family's okay, and protect them. I just can't sleep until we receive a call from them. Just let them be okay, I ask of you." At that moment, nothing mattered any more—not school or work. Then around midnight, the phone rang. My mother answered after the first ring. It was my aunt! She was okay. The whole house jumped and celebrated like it was someone's birthday.

My aunt said that most of our family was fine, but a couple people were missing. They were eventually found, but in the wake of disaster, they had lost their homes. Most of my family members were scattered along the plains, staying in the tents that the United States relief set up for them, while others stayed with relatives in places where the earthquake did not do much damage. I could breathe a sigh of relief for my family. I knew that our family was blessed. I knew other people who were less fortunate and lost family members in the disaster.

To this day, Haiti is still receiving help and aid through many donations. Many kids who lost families will be adopted by new families and will be taken to the United States. What I still have trouble comprehending sometimes is why God allowed a disaster of this magnitude to occur. Why did it take this disaster to make people aware of Haiti and how much we needed help? I remembered Ecclesiastes 3, where God (through Solomon) said that there is a time for everything—a time for every activity under heaven. It may be possible that God allowed this to happen so that Haiti can learn to turn to God once again and lay aside their pins, dolls, groves, idols, and whatever things tie them to voodoo. It is possible that God allowed this to happen so He can teach us how to help and be there for others when they need us.

I want to take the time in this book to thank CNN, the Red Cross, and countless other organizations that stepped up to the occasion, as well as President Obama and the rest of the world leaders who responded to this international emergency. The work that they have done is not just a small act of kindness. Whether a person donated clothes or adopted children or just sent a $5 text donation to YELE (an organization founded by Wyclef Jean), whatever they did was not only to the benefit of the mother land, but also to the glory of the Lord and Savior Jesus Christ. Together we have shown that *"l'union fait la force."*

Growing Up in Haiti: My Parents

If it hadn't been for my parents, Jean and Lineda Beausejour, who brought me up in the gospel and ministry of Christ, I would not be here writing and impacting those around me. These two people—bound by their love, commitment, and most of all, their dedication to Jesus Christ—took the time and effort to mold me into the man I am today.

My father, Jean Claude Beausejour, was born on November 2, 1960 in the city of Tiburon, Haiti, which is south of the capital city of Port-au-Prince. When my father was growing up, another Jean Claude, "Baby Doc," took over the presidential office. As a boy, my father loved to play soccer, which was the national sport in Haiti. As a matter of fact, it's *still* the national sport in Haiti. Soccer was more than just a pastime to Haitians—it was a way of life, and my father was one of the best. He played soccer from the time he was a toddler to when he was in high school. Jean's father was a soldier who served in Haiti's army, so his father was never around during his childhood. My father would often describe the life his father lived, moving around from base to base, meeting different women, and working on many drill exercises.

As a result, Jean grew up with his mother, who worked as a tailor. He learned most of his family values through his mother. The thing that baffled me the most was that my father was born out of wedlock. For some reason, Jean's father wasn't exactly a fan of settling down and living with a wife in a big house complete with a backyard, outdoor swimming pool, and a dog named Fido. So as a boy, my father cooked, cleaned, and fixed things in the house that needed to be fixed. But he still had time to be a regular teen boy, too. Jean loved to play marbles as a kid, and he would play with some of the kids that lived down his block. But then these kids grew restless of just playing for fun and decided to raise the stakes. One day my father came down to the usual block to join his friends as always. Then his friends started betting him and threatened to take whatever he had whenever he lost the game. That was enough. My father dropped the marbles and went home. He never played that game again, for he knew that if you lost any games in that area, people would want to be paid in full—swift and quick. He returned home and continued his quiet, decent life. Then tragedy struck.

When Jean was seventeen, his beloved mother passed away. It must have been agonizing for Jean to lose the only parent who was actually there for him—the one he could turn to for assistance. But he turned to someone else—Jesus Christ. My father was saved at the age of fourteen, but he didn't start to minister until later on in his lifetime. Motivated by the wayward attitude of his fellow brothers and the loss of his mother, Jean began to turn to God for all his needs. The transformation of Jean also reached his siblings while he was growing up. His brother, Pressoir Beausejour, accepted the Lord as his personal Savior and joined a gospel group named Ebenezer. Pressoir played guitar and produced some of the songs that the group sang. I remember when I was growing up, my father would play the record or videotape of the group, and I would look on in awe and amazement as my uncle's fingers seemed to sweep gracefully through the strings. Because of him, I actually envisioned myself playing the guitar too—that wasn't the way it turned out, but it's okay.

In 1980, Jean packed his bags and boarded a plane heading to New York. He did not have the intention of staying in New York, but it's funny how even when we don't intend to do some things in life, God is the driver. He alone knows what our future holds, so the only thing we can do is go with the flow. That's exactly what my father did. He stayed with his father, who subsequently moved to New York. Together, they resided in Astoria, Queens, and Jean's father would attempt to recapture the years that he missed with his son while he was in the Army. Jean and his father would come to an understanding as father and son can—but no amount of time could make up for missing most of a son's childhood. Take the Word of God, for example.

In Luke 15, Jesus tells the parable of the lost son. Basically, a father had two sons, and he gave each son a bit of his property. The younger son, being a little more impatient, demanded that the father give him his share. As soon as he received it, he spent the money on riotous living. When the son had spent all his money and was forced to work in the field feeding pigs, he was so hungry because of the famine that had taken over the land that he was tempted to eat the food laid out for the pigs. Then the son came to his senses and decided to return to his father's house, where he knew there was food in abundance. As soon as father and son met, the father ran and embraced his son, because he was so overjoyed that his son was found. Sometimes it must have hurt my father, knowing that he did not have a father that he can run to.

When I read that story, it makes me feel like no matter where I am or what I'm doing, I will always have a heavenly Father to run to. There are times when we don't speak to Him as much as we should or we don't give Him as much attention as we should, but He is at the end of the field, waiting for us to come and embrace Him. Time won't make up for what you've already missed, but it is never too late to be reconciled to your heavenly Father. Just as the son knew that his father's house was abundant with food, we must come to that same realization that God's love is abundant. Psalm 136:1 says, "His love endures forever." I thank God for my father, because even though he had a hard childhood and suffered loss so young in life, these events shaped him into the man he is today. Don't wait for Father's day to tell your father that you love him. Go out and extend your love to him.

The year was 1983. Jean's father, Pressoir Joseph Beausejour, stood before the congregation of the Rock of Jacob Haitian Church in Queens, New York. His past was filled with deception and estrangement from his children. He now speaks to the young people of Christ so they won't walk down the same road. Pressoir's deep, rich voice seems to ring deep inside every man and woman in the assembly.

In the front row, there was a woman who was listening to the words that proceeded out of the mouth of one of Haiti's finest soldiers. Just like Pressoir's son Jean, this woman had her share of tragedy throughout the years of her life. Her name was Lineda Danois. And yes, you guessed it—she is now my mother. Born on February 5, 1963 in the city of St. Marc (located west of Port-au-Prince), Lineda was different than all the other girls growing up in her time. She didn't like to play with dolls; she didn't spend time going to slumber parties or stay up all night discussing boys or makeup. Lineda possessed a strong personality, bred by being the oldest female sibling in the family. Being the third child of seven, with two older brothers, she would make sure her younger siblings woke up in the morning and got to school on time. She would even cook for them and walk them to the bus stop. Lineda's mother, Precieuse Dortilus, worked as a vendor and a part-time farmer, cultivating crops and raising animals to sell. Her father, Harris Danois, was a carpenter who designed beautiful chairs, tabletops, and other types of furniture. At her school, Lineda would be the one who would help her teachers and professors by performing tasks in the classroom and making sure everything was in good shape. Even though her strong yet humble, helpful lifestyle did not make her too many friends, she was true to herself and God.

On August 28, 1983, Lineda migrated to Queens, New York, looking to escape Haiti's governmental demise. Lineda's parents remained in Haiti, and she lived with her mother's sister in Astoria, Queens. She found a church home in Bethany Baptist Church in Jamaica, Queens. She was part of a mission team that traveled from church to church to sing, evangelize, and minister in different areas around the tri-state area. Some of her visits were at the Rock of Jacob church in Astoria, where Jean and his father went.

Lineda, impressed by Pressoir's preaching, met Pressoir after the service, and he told her about Jean. She would not meet Jean that day, because Jean led a busy life, working and going to school. But in 1985, Lineda and Jean would finally meet. At first they were acquaintances—you know, not so serious. But as they talked about their background and described each other's experiences growing up in Haiti, there was something more than just friendship developing. In early 1986, Jean and Lineda were out having dinner, and Lineda noticed that Jean seemed a little on edge. Jean wanted to tell Lineda that he wanted to take their relationship to the next level, but he wasn't sure how to tell her. Stammering and looking for words, Jean was drowning. Lineda finally told him, "Jean, if you have something to tell me, go ahead and tell me." So Jean told her that the last few months with her had been the best moments of his life, and that he would like to spend the rest of his life with her.

Lineda, taken by Jean's honesty, accepted his engagement.

Lineda and Jean were married on May 24, 1986, and the ceremony was performed in Bethany Baptist Church —the church I would attend during my childhood. To me, this wasn't just a chance meeting or a blind date of any kind. This was actual, true love at its best—true love that may seem only a fairy tale in today's world. When you look at today's marriages, more than half end in divorce. In truth, this is sad, because this is not how God ordained marriage. In Genesis 2:24, God says, "For this reason a man will leave his father and mother and be united to his wife and they will become one flesh." Divorce not only rips this one flesh apart, but also tears the home apart and it leaves a future of uncertainty for both the husband and wife. If a man is blessed with a wife, he must value her. Speaking as an eligible bachelor, sometimes men tend to look for wives on their own. These men feel that they can find the person without consulting God or praying for the right one to come by. Women have the tendency to pick out men based on physique. If both men and women put their faith in God, He will lead them to the right partner.

Later on in Genesis 24:9, Abraham sent his servant, Eliezer, to look for a wife for his son, Isaac. Eliezer set out on his journey, and when he arrived at his destination, he did not ask the town locals or go to the nearest 12 BC-bar to pick up a wife. He kneeled down and prayed to God to bring him a woman suitable for Isaac. The moment he finished praying, a woman named Rebekah came and gave Eliezer's camels water. By Rebekah's good nature and charm, the servant knew that this was the right woman.

I'm not telling you to use your parents or to have your parents choose the right spouse for you. The point of this passage is to tell you to allow God to be the ultimate decision-maker in your life—especially when it comes to something as serious as marriage. Pray for God to send you the right woman or man, and God will always provide. It may not be at your time—but God wants us to be patient and have faith in Him. Lineda and Jean did not meet by chance; God had ordained the meeting. He had orchestrated all the events that occurred throughout their lives up to the day and year they met. And I am happy to say that they are still going strong—even after twenty-four years.

If you are currently married and you want to keep your marriage going strong, just remember two things: trust God, and trust your spouse. Trust God, because if there is no God in the relationship, there is no love or truth. To put it plainly, Jesus is love; Jesus is truth. Love and truth shape and mold the relationship of a man and woman. Trust your spouse, because from the moment you say "I do," you are physically and eternally tied to that person. I'm not trying to wear you fellas down—but whatever your wife feels, her husband must feel. Whatever struggles you go through, your spouse has to be by your side to walk with you when the roads get treacherous.

Nobody said marriage was going to be easy. Nobody said being a Christian was going to be easy, either—but do we stand alone and try to withstand all the obstacles that Satan throws our way? No—at least I hope not! We bond with our fellow Christians and fight what Paul calls the "principalities of evil" (Ephesians 6:12). Divorce is a principality of evil, and it's a force that is sadly winning, year after year. The marriage of Lineda and Jean Beausejour is a true testimony that if you wait and pray, the right person will come to you, and you both will truly live happily ever after—not just after the marriage, but after this life, as well. If you put Jesus Christ at the center of your marriage and put your trust in Him no matter how many problems you go through on earth, the reward is more than fitting in heaven. When we get to heaven, we shall all behold God in His glory and splendor. God's presence will be beyond our wildest imagination—beyond what we can envision. But it has to be what *you* envision. God gave us free will and free choice. So let's *will* ourselves to make the *choice* of following Jesus—the son of God who has set us all *free*.

PART 2

Growing Up

"When I was a child, I talked like a child, I thought like a child I reasoned like a child. When I became a man, I put childish ways behind me"

(1 Corinthians 13:11)(NIV).

CHAPTER 2

Behind the Words: Growing Up

It Wasn't Easy

It wasn't easy being born in the Empire State,
Growing up every day with little food on my plate
It wasn't easy being abused at the age of three
when a teacher severely beat me to the third degree
It wasn't easy walking through snow up to my waist
or having chicken pox stubble on my face.
It wasn't easy drowning in a pool six feet deep
or hearing outside noises so loud that I couldn't sleep
It wasn't easy learning that I have a permanent head scar
courtesy of running too far and banging that fence bar
It wasn't easy being clowned and frowned on at school
because I didn't wear designer gear and wasn't cool
It wasn't easy when they hassled me for not being tall
so I couldn't ball with the big boys at all.
Most of all, it was never, ever easy when I moved south
People stared at me strange because I had a different mouth
It wasn't easy experiencing racism for the first time
in my first month of high school in grade nine.
It wasn't easy fighting for every credit just to graduate
or applying to college at the last possible date
When I had a chance to know and grow with my best friend
It wasn't easy finding out that he's now in the state pen
It wasn't easy making a decision to write for anyone but myself
especially when I feel like sticking my poems on some high shelf
By now you can probably see, it's not easy being me
But I make it work for me; I strive to succeed
I learn how to make a promise of a future more guaranteed
Life is hard so I can learn how to stand on my own two feet.

I know, I know—I'm negative about my childhood. You may ask why I highlight only the low points of my early life in my piece. Was it my goal to make my readers feel sorry for me? No. My goal was to let you know that the events you have read about actually shaped me into the person I am today. If none of those things had happened, I wouldn't be here, writing poems to inspire and motivate people everywhere. As you can see, my childhood was rough. Even though my parents tried to make it as bearable as possible, I couldn't avoid the cuts and bruises that everyday life gave me. But that's okay. Just like the last line of my poem said, life is hard so I can learn how to stand on my own two feet. Life *has* to be difficult so you can learn diligence and perseverance through failing. Learning through your failures helps you to be a better individual the next day. Growing up was hard, but I also had some great moments. It helped that God has placed me around some of the most caring, charismatic characters to learn from.

I was born in Queens, New York on July 28, 1987 in what was then Queens General Hospital in College Point, right near Jamaica Ave. Currently I am the oldest of three brothers, but for seven and a half years, I was an only child. It was lonely, but that was probably one of the reasons that my parents (dare I say it?) *spoiled* me. Well, not really spoiled—but I usually got what I wanted every birthday and Christmas. Throughout everything I had, however, my parents taught me a very important thing early on. Things were not just given to you. You had to earn them. So they would monitor my schoolwork and my progress in terms of doing house chores. If I performed well in school and did all my work, I was blessed with certain privileges. If not, I was blessed with something *else*—something a little less pleasurable—as a child. And when I misbehaved, I would be bestowed with so many *blessings* that it would hurt to sit down for a few days!

When I was only three years old, I experienced firsthand what may be known today as child abuse. I was in my daycare program, and one of the assistant teachers called me. I came to her, and she noticed that my shoes were untied. She told me to bend down to tie my shoes. *What?* I was only three years old. I could barely tie a knot. I sat there, fiddling with my laces, and she got impatient. Next thing I knew, I felt a sharp pain on my shoulders. Cringing in pain, I look up. It was the assistant teacher, and she had a menacing look on her face. In her right hand, she had a long yardstick. Then she struck again. Then she hit me some more. The details are fuzzy, because I was so young at the time—but even as a three-year-old I remembered how embarrassed and hurt I was. The worst thing is that I don't even remember if I told my mother about the incident or not. She later told me I did, and she went and talked with the assistant teacher about it.

For a long time, I wished that my mother had done more than just *talk* to her. I wanted that lady to pay. I wanted her locked away. Then a divine thing happened. When I was in middle school, I was walking home, and I passed the daycare center on the way home. Surprisingly, she was *still* working as a teacher there. She saw me, smiled, and said, "Marc, how are you doing? My, have you grown!" At first, I didn't want to say anything to her. To me, she hadn't changed a bit. I could still see her man-like hands holding the yardstick, whipping me like a stray dog. But something was different about her. She seemed *happy* to see me. I was confused. Was this the same teacher that beat me back in the day? It couldn't be.

"I'm doing good, ma'am," I said. I found out that she had been saved—born again—and she was not the same mean person she was before. From that day forward, I learned never to hold a grudge against a person (especially for years), because at that very moment, God could be working in their hearts. When we are saved, we become new in Christ. The "old has passed away, behold all things are new" (2 Corinthians 5:17). I hope she is doing well wherever she is. I know that God is watching over her.

The years 1994 and 1995 must have been the most eventful years of my life. In 1993, my parents left Rock of Jacob Church and continued to go to Bethany French Baptist Church in Jamaica, Queens full time. At that time, the church had an after-school program that my mother signed me up to attend. Every couple days, my mother's friend would drop me off at the church after school. When I attended the program, it was hard for me to make friends at first, because these were all kids who went to *public* school. These kids were not exactly rough, but I'm sure they knew how to handle themselves on Jamaica Ave. As for me, I was still attending a Catholic school. Kids were nice, they didn't do anything to each other, and they respected their elders. It may not seem like much of a difference, but to us, it was like we lived in two different *worlds*. The older kids ridiculed me. Some of the girls made fun of my slight build and skinny frame.

I was prepared for all the laughing and jeering, but what I wasn't prepared for was the trip we took to a park pool in Manhattan. All the older kids were showing off, diving and splashing one another. I preferred not to swim (since I didn't know how), and I stood at the pool's edge, talking to some friends. Suddenly one of the older kids (I don't know if he was joking or not) came from behind and pushed me into the pool. This wasn't just two or three feet of water; this was the *deep end*. I was thrashing about, yelling "Help me!" every time my head bobbed above water. The kid who pushed me was just standing there, laughing. *No one's going to help me,* I thought. I was taking in gulps of nasty chlorinated water, and I could sense myself blacking out. The next thing I knew was the feeling of big hands wrapping around my body. I was out of the pool. One of the kid's friends finally realized that it was not a joke, and he dove in after me. The pool attendant told me to stay near the restrooms and just take a breath for a little while. I didn't go back to the pool that day.

For a while, I thought everything would be all right—no more drama. Then something else happened. In the 1994–1995 school year, my mother transferred me to the local public school, Public School 50, due to the high prices of the Catholic school admission. I wasn't too sure about this change, because I had a lot of friends at my Catholic school, and I knew leaving was not going to be easy. But I was also open to it. Finally I would be able to relate to the kids hanging out on Jamaica Ave. Finally I would be accepted into the "cool" circle.

The bad thing was that it would take years for me to be really accepted, and that first year was difficult. In my very first day, I was "initiated" into P.S. 50, and my initiation test was to see how many punches I could take from a local bully, and his boys. At the end of this test, I was bruised up, my shoes had been taken off my feet, and my clothes were disheveled.

In 1995, in my second semester, I was at recess when a kid named Joel started giving me a hard time. I don't remember what he said, but somewhere inside, a spark burned. There was a sandy area near the asphalt where I was sitting, and without warning, I threw sand in Joel's face. Joel got angry—then I realized how tall he was. So I started running as fast as I could. Mind you, I was a very fast runner, and I left Joel in my dust. Nothing could stop me as I stared back at Joel, who was yards behind me—nothing except the fence post I didn't see ahead of me. *Wham!* All I heard next was the ringing sound of metal against a thick-headed skull. Talk about being a bonehead. Trust me—I was the biggest bonehead around. I was rushed to Jamaica Hospital, where the doctors stitched up my head. It was painful, and I was stuck wearing a bandage wrap around my head for about a week or two. Since then, I've always been very careful at recess, and watched where I was going when I ran. I still have a scar where my head was stitched. I could have looked at it and been angry that the scar had deformed me—but instead, I thank God for teaching me a lesson in restraint. Even though I banged my head and lost more blood than I ever would again, there's no denying that I learned my lesson.

The rest of public school went by without any major incident. I passed all my classes, graduated from the sixth grade, and prepared myself for middle school. As far as sports go, I always thought I was athletically inept because of my skinny frame and stature. I could play soccer, because my father and I had played plenty of times, but that was about it. I couldn't play anything else, unless you counted street games we played, like handball and a game called suicide (don't ask me about the name)—but I sure couldn't play basketball then. However, I knew that in order for me to even survive at Junior High School 217, I had to play basketball. I started by watching street players play in parks, and I remember the motion of the ball, the fluid movements of the players as they set picks, and the strength and tenacity needed to finish off a play with a dunk. I was sucked in, but I was discouraged, because I was always too short to play.

Every day after school, if I was waiting for a ride from my parents (who were finally blessed with a Honda Civic), the school janitors, who were very cool, would lend me a basketball and the keys to the gym so I could work on my game. I would be in there for an hour every day, working on my jump shot, hook shots, and vertical jump. When my friends and I played pickup games, I started with my defense. I would block so many of their shots that if a player saw me coming, he would rather pass the ball than take a chance by shooting in front of me. A biblical lesson I can take from this experience is that God has blessed each of us with individual talents. Sometimes we must believe through *faith* that we are each talented in something—one way or the other. Do we utilize God's gifts when He blesses us with them, or do we sit and waste our gifts?

It took me a while to realize that my true gift was in writing poems and skits. If you have a talent, don't hesitate to use your talent for the glory of Jesus Christ, because you will be storing up treasures in heaven when you use your talents for God.

Goin' South

I think that the turning point in my life was when I moved from Queens, New York to Kennesaw, Georgia in the summer of 2001. I had just graduated from the eighth grade at Junior High School 217, and I was enjoying my summer and anticipating the first year of high school at Hillcrest. This was considered a rough school by many, but at least that was where my friends were going. In July of 2001, my parents and one of their friends took a cruise to the Bahamas, leaving my brothers and me under the care of one of their church friends. On the way to Florida, where my parents would board the Carnival ship, they passed by Georgia and noticed how beautiful and quiet it was. It stood in contrast to where we were living in Richmond Hill, New York. Just like many other people from urban areas who were attracted by the quiet Southern life and Southern hospitality down there, my parents couldn't resist.

When they returned from their cruise, my parents did not make their intentions to move known until late July—just before my birthday. I remember it like it was yesterday. It was Friday, and my mother and I were at a Laundromat. It was there my mother told me that we were moving. I couldn't believe it. There was just no way we were moving. This was my *home*—my friends, my future, and my whole *life* were in the Big Apple, the mecca of basketball. I looked at my mother in shock and confusion. I don't think I said another word on the way home from the Laundromat. My mother has always hinted at how much she did not like the school system and how much she wanted to move. But I was thinking that we were just moving to another borough—probably to Long Island or something—but certainly not leave the *state*.

The month before I moved was the hardest for me. I was told not to tell anyone we were moving until our final week in New York, and it ripped me up inside. I remember when I was younger, I used to take going to Bethany French Baptist Church for granted—but I was fourteen at the time, and I cherished every last moment that I was there. What hurt the most was when Bethany made the annual announcement for the youth retreat in the first weekend of September. I had attended the previous year, and I had my hopes set on going there again—but it was not going to happen. Finally, the second week of August arrived, and our apartment looked like we had just moved in. Everything was packed away, the closets were empty, and the floors were clean. I went to Friday night Bible study at Bethany, expecting another regular Friday. But when I got there, I saw a big cake on a table near the kitchen, and the cake read, "We'll miss you, Marc." My friends in New York may not remember it now, but that gesture really showed me that they cared about me. From that moment forward, the youth of Bethany, deacons, and pastors always held a special place in my heart. I was truly blessed to have grown up in their ministry, and it shaped me into the type of leader I am and still strive to be.

After we said our good-byes, my mother, my two little brothers, and I boarded a Greyhound bus, and we were on our way to Atlanta. I looked longingly at the tall skyscrapers and buildings that highlighted New York, and I vowed that I would come back. But at the time, I could only look ahead to a new life in Georgia.

It was about 3:00 or 4:00 in the morning when we arrived in Atlanta, Georgia, and my mother's friend (who had attended Bethany and moved to Georgia three years before) took us to his home. We stayed in his house from August of 2001 until May of 2002. During that time, I started my freshman year at Kennesaw Mountain High School in Kennesaw, Georgia. I hated it. At the time I attended, the school was only in its second year of existence, so it was a pretty new school—the hallways were clean, there was no graffiti in the bathrooms, and there were no condoms or magazines on the floor. Everything was Mr. Clean-new.

I don't know if it was because the school was so new, but the kids there were arrogant. I have never seen so many stuck-up kids in one place, and the older upperclassmen picked on the freshman. The fact that I was not only a freshman but also a new kid gave them the right to say and do what they wanted. But by this time, I'd had it with all the picking on and the clowning. I was from Queens, New York. I had to *represent*.

Kennesaw Mountain High School was predominantly white, and there were only a few black kids there. One white senior came up to me and started giving me a hard time, making fun of my nationality and my color. Anger was building up in me. This guy was three or four inches taller than me, but I didn't care. I envisioned myself punching him squarely in the face. Then my health teacher (who happened to be there) stopped this boy before he could go further with his harassment. At first I was grateful— but then the guy targeted me because he felt I had reported him. I thought, *I didn't tell on you; you were dumb enough to get caught.* Because I was scared, I started cutting classes, and I was falling behind in class. When I did attend, it was when we had a test, which I usually failed. This was the last straw.

I really got homesick. One time, I was so homesick, I fell into silent depression. I needed an intervention from God. I needed wisdom and guidance. I couldn't rely on my new friends— especially a friend who ended up taking the wrong road in life and landed someplace he didn't deserve to be. At that time, I needed God to show up *in person.* The only thing I had at my disposal was my writing.

I didn't become a self-proclaimed poet until later in my life. I actually took up writing just to let off some anger and get everything on paper. I wrote poem after poem, and I was reminded of David from the Bible. If you need an example of someone who wrote any time something was bothering him, it was David. 1 Samuel and 2 Samuel highlight David's rise from a humble shepherd to the King of Israel.

When Samuel, the prophet, was called by God to anoint David to be Saul's successor as king, Samuel came to the house of David's father, Jesse, and called all of Jesse's sons. One by one, Jesse's sons appeared before Samuel. Each time Samuel saw one of David's older brothers, who were large in stature and well-built, God would say, "This is not the one." Finally, when Samuel thought every one of Jesse's son's appeared, Jesse told Samuel that he had one more son who was watching the sheep. The Bible does describe David as a good-looking boy, and he was very responsible, but we cannot forget that he was also the *youngest* of

Jesse's sons. David's brothers must have given him a hard time for that, but God still saw greatness in him.

First Samuel 16:7 explains that the Lord does not look at outward appearance, as people do; He looks at the heart. God saw that David had an obedient heart. If David could keep watch over his flocks day and night, David was the right person to watch over God's people. David did not only become one of the greatest kings in the Old Testament, but also a talented poet.

I often dub David "the original poet." His words in the Psalms display his daily conversations with God. Some are about protecting David from his enemies, some are about God being with David in times of hardship, and some ask for forgiveness of sins. When I write poems to inspire others, I like to think of myself as a modern David. I write to edify and glorify God through my words. But as talented as I am in writing poems, there is one thing David had that I seriously lack. Actually, there are a lot of things I lack compared to David, but the biggest characteristic is *faith*. I didn't have the faith I needed, because I wasn't confident through God. Satan basically had me in his web of doubt. I hated my life. I hated my new state. I needed some answers from God.

CHAPTER 3

Internal Struggle, Followed by Redemption

Escape

I'm so sick of the past; life is moving too fast
I feel like an injured arm in need of a cast
I always want a change, but I can never rearrange
a spotless life that always seemed out of range
Jailed like a convict, caged like a bird
Now more than ever, Lord, I need Your holy Word.
Just like David in the desert when fleeing from Saul
My force is diminishing; there's no hope at all.
There are times when I want to stay where I'm at
But I'm constantly under attack; I don't step up to bat.
Lord, I know that my faith is the key
At times, though, I feel that You've left me
The world is deceptive; there are so many stereotypes
As the future of this nation swings in terms of skin types.
Lord, if there's a way to escape, just tell me how
If there was ever a time I needed You, the time is now
I'll trust in You, because I know You're great
One day, You'll help me escape.

Feeling Trapped

I felt like I had hit rock bottom at one point in my life, even though I was only fourteen years old and at the prime of my teen years. My freshman year at Kennesaw Mountain was going to be a bust. I flunked four classes; there was no way I was going to be promoted to the tenth grade. My father, whom I would always go to for advice when I needed guidance, was still in New York. My first two weeks at school were already depressing when the news came that a plane controlled by terrorists had crashed into the World Trade Center. More than ever, I wanted to be in New York. I wanted to feel its pain—to know what was running through the minds of my friends at that moment. I felt displaced, confined, and caged. I needed to escape, just like in the previous poem.

The ironic thing is that I grew up in a family that had trained me to turn to God in times of trouble and pray when I needed guidance. But I did not. You may go so far as to say that in 2001 and 2002, I was at the point of renouncing my faith and just forgetting about the Bible and its promises. Sure, I still went to church. I started to attend Marietta Church of God, which was an American church—but it was one faith with different nationalities. Inside, I was a poser. I looked like I was singing with the congregation. I took part in the Holy Communion every first

Sunday like I usually did when I was in Bethany Baptist Church in New York. But it was all for show.

I hid from the world. I was closed from society inside of me. I did not have the love of Jesus Christ, because I felt that Jesus did not love me. I thought, "If Jesus loved me, then why was I going through so much?" I forgot what Jesus did for me in the past. I forgot that He had saved my life so many times—especially during the 1990s—I could have been dead or permanently disabled. I forgot about the time I accepted Him to be my Lord and Savior and was baptized on April 16, 2001, a few months before I moved to Georgia. I could only think about my present situation and my present pain.

If you read the book of Exodus, following the Israelites' flight from Egypt, you will see that the Israelites wandered in the desert for forty years. It didn't have to be that long, but the people kept grumbling, complaining that there was no water or food and that life would have been better if they were in Egypt. They forgot what God had done for them. God had delivered them and called them His own. The forty years were punishment for disobedience and lack of faith.

Even though I was suffering from a lack of faith at that time, I had enough of a Bible background to know that I couldn't remain the way I was and expect God to work a miracle in my life without believing in Him. All I had was His word. But I was like Doubting Thomas, who did not believe Jesus rose from the dead. I needed *proof.* Little did I know that my proof would come—and it would come abundantly.

The DIRT Crew

I am not one to brag, but I had a lot of God-given talent. I could write poems and lyrics. I knew my Bible more than any kid my age would, I was the son of a deacon, and I was a missionary for Christ. My problem was that I did not know how to utilize my skills and abilities for God. I needed someone to push me and to take the place of my father when it came to ministry and discipline. God provided me that leader in the person of Brother Barry Dollar. During my freshman year in high school, while my parents were still attending Marietta Church of God, I started to go to Eastwood Baptist Church across the street from Marietta Church of God. I know it's wrong to compare churches, but I couldn't help noticing that Eastwood seemed like a church that meant and practiced what they preached. And in addition to that, they had a much better youth base.

Brother Barry Dollar was the youth pastor of Eastwood at the time, and he held youth services every Wednesday in one of the rooms above the church gym. Barry and I met after a Sunday night youth program called AWANA (Approved Workmen Are Not Ashamed). Barry was not in charge of the AWANA program, but the AWANA leaders were the ones who introduced me to him. My first impression was, "This guy's tall!" Then my second impression was that this man may be who God had sent to reaffirm my faith in Christ and help me flourish.

Barry invited me to attend Wednesday night youth Bible study, and from that time forward, I started to put my life back together. Despite my dismal grades at school, I picked it up and passed my remaining courses. Kennesaw Mountain, being a strict school, decided that I had to be retained in the ninth grade because of my poor GPA. But I was going to get a blessing in disguise. My mom came to me and gave me the news that we were moving to our own house, which was outside the district of Kennesaw Mountain High School. My father would come back around the end of April to finalize the deal. In May of 2001, we settled into our nice, new ranch home near the Acworth District. Now I could attend another high school—North Cobb High School.

At the beginning of the following year, North Cobb looked at my transcript and came to the conclusion that I would *not* be held back in ninth grade. I was overjoyed. Even though it meant retaking the courses I failed the year before, my transcript still said I was a *sophomore!* God has given me another chance to start fresh and turn my future in Georgia in *my* favor. During this time, our youth group at Eastwood was growing so large that the small rooms we held our Wednesday night studies in were getting crowded. Eastwood funded the construction of a facility that would combine two and three rooms together and make one youth hangout spot, complete with pool tables, video games, and music. This location was dubbed "the Attic," and when it was complete, Barry's vision of the DIRT (Disciples In Real Time) Crew ministry started to become a reality. Finally, with my school problems behind me, my inner doubt leaving me, and a substantial youth group that I have not been around with since the youth base I left back in New York, I was ready to take off. I was learning more from Brother Barry's preaching, and I started to take my personal Bible study more seriously.

Brother Barry also believed in displaying and sharing talents, so he started to hold open mic nights on the last Wednesday of every month, and people were singing, dancing, playing instruments, and even rapping. It was my first open mic, and I was nervous. I sat holding my poem in my hand, my knees shaking and teeth chattering. Finally, it was my turn. I got up on stage and read my poem. When I was done, the Attic exploded. Brother Barry said, "Congrats on getting a standing O, man!" Usually when you got a standing O, your performance was incredible. I remember going to sleep happy that night, and I said, "Thank You, God. I know now that I should have never doubted You, and I'm sorry I didn't listen to You. Thank You for testing me and then helping me through the test in the end." It was a tunnel that seemed long and dark, and there seemed to be no hope. But there's always a light at the end of this tunnel.

There really is a light at the end of the tunnel—*our* light at the end of the tunnel. Jesus is the source of the light, but we have to trust in Him so we can turn our light on and let people see the light and life of Christ. Matthew 5:16 says, "Let your light shine before men, that they may see your good deeds, and praise your Father in Heaven." God has allowed my light to shine in my darkest tunnel, and I have finally escaped from within myself.

DIRT Crew's Story

Each of us, at one point in life, wants to stand out for a particular reason. One reason could be that for a particular skill or talent that only a few people possess. Another reason is simply for the extra attention that a person gets from standing out as an *individuals.* Let's face it—we all want to be noticed above others for one reason or another. I know I did.

When I was a kid living in Richmond Hill, New York, my favorite animated movie was *A Goofy Movie,* which starred Goofy (of course) and his son, Max. Max was a character I related to at the time, because in the beginning of the movie, all Max cared about was being *accepted* by the rest of his school peers. He would even risk getting into serious trouble to get that kind of attention. The movie was also a musical (like all classic Disney movies were—that's what made them classics!), and one of the songs Max sang was "Stand Out." I can still see the scene where his friends and his once-hostile schoolmates cheered him after he pulled a prank on the principal and did an in-school auditorium concert, depicting his favorite singer, Powerline. Max would skateboard home singing, "I'm gonna stand out till you notice me." I looked at the screen, and I felt like Max and I were one and the same. I wanted to stand out. I was sick of being picked on for my slight build. I was sick of being used and taken for granted. I wanted to do something that would *make* people notice me. Then that's when personal pride set in, and I did not think about the people I was hurting or trying to transform myself for. All I could see at the time was myself—who else but me?

Joining the DIRT Crew ministry in 2002 taught me first and foremost that it wasn't all about me. Brother Barry Dollar built the spiritual foundation of this ministry based on John 13. In this chapter, Jesus got up from the table after supper, took off His robe, and wrapped a towel around His waist. He then poured water into a basin and began washing His disciples' feet. Just imagine that ... the Son of God—the Everlasting Father; the Prince of Peace; the Wonderful Counselor; the fourth man who appeared in the burning furnace next to Shedrach, Meshach, and Abednego; the Lamb of God; the Alpha and Omega—stooping low to wash the feet of his disciples. These feet were *dirty* and probably smelly. Not only were they dirty with dust, mud, and grass, but also dirty with sin.

None of us are without sin. We have all sinned. Without the blood of Jesus Christ, to God, we are *all* dirty. But Jesus shows us a classic example of humbling Himself to be a servant. Forget who you are and serve others.

As Jesus started to was the feet of this friends, one of His disciples, Peter, opposed this, wondering why the Lord was washing *their* feet. Peter did not want Jesus to wash his feet—not because he was not thankful for what Jesus was doing, but because He did not want to think of his master being a humble, lowly servant. Jesus then replied, "But if I don't wash your feet, you won't belong to me."

Peter then says, "Then wash my hands and head as well Lord, not just my feet."(John 13:9)(NIV) The verse that probably summarizes this whole passage is John 13:14, which is what

DIRT Crew stands on. Jesus says, "Since I, the Lord and Teacher, have washed your feet, you ought to wash each other's feet." As Christians and as people, we must learn to leave our comfort zones and serve others—just as Christ has served us. Life shouldn't just be all about *us*. The world does not revolve around *us*. You may be a movie star, a millionaire, or a politician (crooked or honest)—it does not matter. What matters is that we must lay aside ourselves and be servants to others.

Brother Barry dedicated not only his ministry to this, but also his life. As an ambassador, pastor, and missionary, he constantly strives to serve others day by day. I have learned much from him about life and scripture. His ministry was the answer when I had questions about myself, such as, *Where do I stand at? What is my goal in life? If I do stand out, am I standing out for the right reasons?* Those questions (and more) were answered the minute I step into the Attic. I had to learn that no matter how much I tried to stand out in life, I could never satisfy *everybody*.

This is true of my book. Some of you may obtain this book, and after reading the first three pages (heck, after reading the preface), slam it shut and thrust it back onto the shelf, put it back in the box, or give it back to the friend who let you read it on your free time. And that's absolutely fine with me. My goal is not to impress people or stand out for my works. I don't want to stand *out;* rather, I want to stand *beside* people. I want to stand beside fellow believers. I want to help other people achieve a common goal—the goal of getting a closer relationship with God. It's not for me, but for the glory of the Most High. Through Brother Barry, Jesus has spoken to me. He has addressed me to stand beside *Him*—and if I do want to stand out, stand out *for Him*.

Let's try to stand out for Jesus every day when we get a chance to. Let's serve others, just as Christ served us, and save, just as He saved.

CHAPTER 4

Though I Walk ...

Walking through the Valley of Death

Pounding drums
The terrified yells of a few hundred civilians
A young boy sprinting barefoot at the sound
he has no shoes, so the pebbles tore through soft flesh
But even through pain, he escapes the dreadful drums
Drums signal the end of all happiness—all freedom of choice
The boy sees his cousin, and together, they join others
For a deep pilgrimage through the Sudan, the Valley of Death
The boy's stomach rumbles with hunger, demanding sustenance
Accommodations were so bleak, he would eat leaves.
Wild, poisonous berries and even mud were considered delicacies
The boy's stomach growled in protest as it ejaculated the contents
Painful sores grow and develop around the boy's mouth
In the distance, there is a noise much more feared than drums
A sight more frightful than a million Islamic armed soldiers
Sharp, malevolent teeth stared at the boys as they crush and snap
A lion charged as the boys stood their ground
waving sticks to deter and resist the king of beasts.
They boys must stand united, because separation for
a stray, lost boy makes an easy prey for the carnivorous monster.
Forever they march, the blood from their feet wetting the dirt
Reddening the dirt with their perseverance and struggle for survival
Finally, the camp at Ethiopia lies ahead—a heaven at last
The boys have survived the Valley of Death
with the aid the great and powerful Creator. the *Nhialic.*

A Story of Survival

The heat is sweltering as you walk across the desert of Sudan. You don't have any clothes except the ones on your back. Your stomach aches, because you haven't eaten in days. You don't even remember the last time you ate. Danger lurks all around you and your friends. Your friends are all you have, because you are now an orphan. Your parents are missing—most likely deceased. The walk through the wilderness is not a walk through the zoo or park. There are no cages to bar you from the wildlife that roam in this African savannah. Lions, hyenas, wolves, and other predators pose a deadly threat to innocent bystanders and those who lag behind in the struggle to survive. In this battle, only the strong survive, but with every step that you take, another pint of survival is being drained from your body. This is how it's going to end—you'll just keep on walking until you can't walk anymore. You are an inch away from death. Death is so close that you can almost feel it, smell it, and taste it.

Imagine going through this as all these thoughts are running through your head. Imagine being removed from your comfort zone and having to fight for everything you have—including your own life. The world seems cruel. The rich seem to enjoy the lavish lifestyles they have, and they are completely oblivious to the fact that a nation is struggling.

The poem that opened this chapter takes us on a journey through the eyes of the lost boys of Sudan. When the tyranny of Islam tore through the country of Sudan, thousands of boys who ranged from twelve to twenty-six years old were forced to flee by foot to refugee camps in Ethiopia. The journey was terrible, and many of the boys in the group did not survive. Not only did they fight bouts of starvation and treacherous heat, but they fought the animals that constantly followed them, waiting for a straggler to fall behind.

One night at a DIRT Crew Bible study, Brother Barry invited a man named Abraham Nhial to the Attic. Abraham is currently a Sudanese pastor who lives in Atlanta, Georgia, but was one of the lost boys who made the pilgrimage from Sudan to Ethiopia. He was about twelve when the Islamic government tore him away from his family, and he was forced to join other orphan boys in the walk of death. Abraham spoke, and I remembered him saying that if it had not been for God, who watched over him throughout this terrible ordeal, he would not be alive today to testify for us.

I met Abraham after the service, and he was lively character—laid back, but also strong in his faith. After the meeting, I felt a strong dislike for continents of power like Europe, Asia, and even the United States for allowing this to happen and not providing quick aid. But that anger soon abated, because I knew that God has a plan for everything that occurred, and all we could do was go with the flow and let it build us, not break us.

When I think back to some events in the past where government rule and monarchies destroyed lives and resulted in the sacrifice of many people, I think about the Native Americans and the long journey they took from Georgia to the Oklahoma Territory, known as the Trail of Tears. The reason the Native Americans were forced out of their lands surprised and angered me more than anything. It was all for gold and property rights given to settlers by the government. I also thought about the Holocaust, where 17 million European Jews would be victims to the ruthless government of Adolf Hitler and the cruelty of the SS officials at the concentration camps. These are prime examples of how government power and money was sought after so much that people did not give any regard to human life whatsoever.

In the Bible, there is another perfect example of corruption. The lands of Judah and Israel were conquered by the Babylonian troops under King Nebuchadnezzar. The people and tribes of Judah, having lost everything, were forced to travel as slaves to the land of Babylon and serve the Babylonians. The story can be found in various locations, including Jeremiah, Lamentations, and Daniel. In Lamentations, Jeremiah is grieving for his people. As a prophet of the Lord, he had warned the Israelites countless times to turn from their sins and turn to God, or God would turn their land into rubble. The people continued their ignorance, and God's Word came to pass. The book of Lamentations, which follow Jeremiah, explains the grief of the prophet for his people. "Jerusalem's streets, once bustling with people, are now silent. Like a widow broken with grief, she sits alone in her mourning" (Lamentations 1:1)(NIV).

In the same sense, Abraham described his homeland being extremely quiet after he returned from a morning activity. He then saw the lifeless bodies of his uncles, aunts, and friends. His family was missing—possibly held as prisoners of war or slain. The silence would forever haunt Abraham, and the sound of the pounding drums, which signaled the arrival of the Islamic government and troops, would stay with him, too. But being a servant of God, he has learned to rely on God despite everything he went through.

Think about Daniel, who was exiled from his home following the Babylonian invasion. He was a slave to the king. He could have turned his back on God because of the situation he went through. But instead, he drew *closer* to God and worked his way up in rank with patience and humility until King Nebuchadnezzar appointed David as one of his top advisors. The book of Daniel is unique. It shows us that when we endure a tough journey, God will be there for us when we need Him. But it also shows that when we begin to take God for granted, He will *remove* us from our comfort zone to teach us a lesson about giving thanks to Him and appreciating Him.

In Daniel 4, Nebuchadnezzar had a dream about a tree that stood in the middle of the earth. The tree was huge, and there were many creatures dwelling in it. Then a messenger—perhaps an angel—came from heaven and ordered the tree to be cut down. The stump remained, bound with iron and bronze, and would have to endure the ravages of weather and animalism. The dream was explained to Daniel, and Daniel told Nebuchadnezzar that *he* represented the tree. The king would be cut off in his prime, driven out of human society, and live like an animal. In time, the dream was fulfilled when the king bragged about how great he was. He was taken away from society to live, eat, and sleep like an animal. Once he acknowledged that God is the great and true God, his kingdom was given back to him, and he was restored. Nebuchadnezzar then gave praise to God and was humbled by his experiences.

During the years I struggled with pride, I considered myself to be a good basketball player. I would brag about my skill and mouth off to anyone who thought they were better. Then God humbled me. In March of 2006, I was playing in the church gym, and I rose up for a dunk. I didn't get up high enough, and I missed the dunk. To make matters worse, I came down awkwardly and heard a pop. My knee felt funny—like it was detached. I had to be helped home that night. After CAT scans and MRIs, I realized that I had a torn ACL. I realized that I was not the greatest after all and that this was a wakeup call from God. I can still play, but not as efficiently as before.

God wants all of us to lean and depend on Him—not only when things are bad for us, but *all* the time. On our good days, we have to thank God for the ability to wake up and eat food. On our bad days, we have to thank God for the same. Life is not always going to be easy and desirable, but just as Abraham Nhial did, we have to draw closer to God. "Trust in the Lord with all your heart; do not depend on your own understanding. Seek his will in all you do and he will direct your paths" (Proverbs 3:5).

CHAPTER 5

Mold Me and Make Me

Make Me; Don't Forsake Me

Lord, take me back to the good old ancient days,
Where I can gaze upon those who have marked their ways.
Make me like Noah, who stood firm against the flood
Against strange, deranged people who knew nothing of the Blood.
Make me like Abraham, a father of a nation so vast
A blessed, promised people whose country would last
Give me the mind of Jacob so I can dream of Your glory
So when I wake the next day, I will have another story
Lord, I ask You to give me a strong, faithful vibe
So I can be a cornerstone of one of the Twelve Tribes
Make me like Moses, so when Pharaoh says, "No,"
I can rebuke and refuse and say, "Let my people go."
Give me his courage—Your power through his staff
So that when enemies laugh, I can unleash Your wrath
Just like Joshua, give me a battle strategy
So I can strive and fight to set Your people free.
Let my faith in You rise to a higher length.
Just like Samson, grant me the power of super strength
Make me like Samuel, a prophet humble and wise
Help me uncover the shroud that hides all lies.
Like David, help me defeat all my fleshly giants.
Help me remain reliant, even when others remain defiant
Make me like Elijah, who was taken and never saw death
Make me like Elisha, whose bones gave a dead man breath
Make me like the kings who served You till the end
Like Daniel, give me peace so I can sleep in the lion's den
Give me the words of Apostle Paul in every letter
So I can persuade every individual to serve You better

Reveal to me what You've revealed to the one You've loved
Give me a sign—a wonder from heaven above.
Make me an example of love through great sacrifice
Allow me to be an image of Your Son, Jesus Christ.
Complete me, rearrange me, make me, and if You must, break me
But Lord, Father God, I ask that You don't forsake me.

The Potter's House

In the last chapter, I mentioned the destruction of Jerusalem by the Babylonians during the time of Jeremiah. After countless warnings to the people about the upcoming judgment through the prophet, the people continued to do evil in the eyes of God. The Israelites rained conviction and punishment on their own heads, and God made them pay. But prior to that event, God instructed Jeremiah to go to the potter's house, and He would continue to speak to Jeremiah there.

When Jeremiah came to the house, the potter was busy at his wheel, making a jar. But the jar did not shape the way the potter wanted, so he squashed the jar into a lump of clay and started again. What was God trying to show Jeremiah? Why did He have Jeremiah watch a potter in the midst of a trial-and-error masterpiece?

God then told Jeremiah, "O Israel, can I not do to you as this potter has done to his clay? As the clay is in the potter's hand, so are you in my hand." (Jeremiah18:6)(NIV) This passage was the inspiration for the previous poem. Sometimes we tend to forget that it was *God* who created us by His image. We tend to put the first four chapters of Genesis in the back of our heads. Why? Because the world would have us believe that we were created by luck and chance. The world would have us believe that an unproven theory such as evolution shapes human beings over the course of time and that there was no divine hand in the creation of the world. If you remember the old time song, "He's Got the Whole World in His Hands," God doesn't have the world in His hands just to be holding it. When I first heard and sang the song as a kid, I always had a vision of God literally holding the world in His hand and keeping it up for ages—sort of like the Greek mythological titan, Atlas, who was forced to bear the world on his shoulders as a punishment. But now I know the bigger picture.

God not only holds the world, but also shapes and controls the events that happen in the world. He knows exactly what is going to take place, whether positive or negative. Everything that occurs in this world is meant to shape our faith and belief in the omnipotent and omnipresent God. God is in control of *everything* that occurs in this world. This may be a bit to take in, because some of us would like to believe that our destiny lies within us— that we can control what happens to us. But that's just not true. Can we see what will happen in our future? Can we see what will even happen tomorrow? Today? In the next few minutes? In the next few seconds? No, we can't see that—but God can. All we can really do is rely on Him and be the people He knows we can be.

I wrote the previous poem when I thought of how God showed Jeremiah the example of the potter reshaping his jar to make it into a shape that he desired. I wanted God to do the same for *me*. I wanted God to shape me, and if there was a part of me He didn't like, then I wanted Him to correct me and reshape me into a vessel that could be used for Him.

As time passed, I was making strides at the DIRT Crew ministry at Eastwood,. I was meditating on the Word, our youth group went to mission projects around Atlanta, and we were making a difference in people's lives by showing the love of Christ to others. I liked where I was, but I was not where I wanted to be. I continued to serve, over and over, time after time, without complaint—but I wanted to serve a bigger role. I knew I had to be patient and wait on God, but I was getting older. In 2005, I had been a member of the crew for four years. I don't know about anyone else, but I considered myself to be a veteran student in the ministry. And to top it all off, I just graduated high school (I know, I'm putting too many credentials on myself)! I wanted something *more*. I now know that if I had been a little more patient and waited on God at *His* time, then I would have had more success earlier in other endeavors.

But nonetheless, a blessing did come in the person of Brian Lee, a former youth minister at First Baptist of Atlanta. Brian and another brother, Chris Galloway, started coming over to our youth programs. They played DVDs called *Way of the Master* on the first Wednesday of every month. *Way of the Master* was a show that included author and evangelist Ray Comfort and actor Kirk Cameron. The presentations were mostly on values and knowledge about how to witness Christ to others by using the Ten Commandments as a mirror to show them that they were sinners in the eyes of God and needed a savior. Brian also took our youth group to witness in the streets of Atlanta, which was a very good experience for me, because I became much more open to people. I was using the Word to assist me in my witnessing.

Brother Barry Dollar would later resign as youth director of Eastwood Baptist to expand the DIRT Crew ministry to other churches across the United States, including churches in California, Tennessee, and Alabama. Our youth group leader post was given to Brian Lee, and he did an excellent job of getting the youth involved. He was a lively character. He would poke fun at other students, but he did it out of love. He even got me a couple times! But overall, he is an anointed brother in Christ, and he served as my mentor for a couple years. God was going to use

Brian to shape me into the outspoken leader that I wanted to be for Christ. I allowed myself to be taught by Brian Lee, and Brian used God's Word and his charisma to reshape me into a leader in the DIRT Crew.

Before long, at every Wednesday meeting, Brian gave me the responsibility of opening up services at the Attic. This helped build my confidence so I could continue to be exposed to public speaking and crowds. At first it bothered me. I had bouts where my hand shook uncontrollably on stage and I just stood without any animation and spoke in a monotone voice. The first few months were tough. But then the experience and faith in God built my confidence, and I slowly became the leader I wanted to be—and that God wanted me to be. Brian would then appoint me, Reggie Brun, Tony Gress, and Reggie Rowe to be youth leaders for the middle school and high school groups. Later on, some of my other friends, Michael Bell, Cynthia Brun, Michelle Brun, Steven Brun, Bria Haynes, Shaun Tenney, and his wife, Jenna would be leaders as well. I had the great pleasure of working with these great brothers and sisters in Christ, and I want them to know that each of them had an impact on my journey through life and my spiritual relationship with Christ. Together, we allowed God to mold us together into a cohesive unit for Him, and we continue that work until this day.

I think back to all the leaders in the Bible and can't help but think that before they became leaders, they had to fight doubt within themselves and get over it to serve God. What made it more amazing was that life was even tougher for them. Back in biblical times, there was no modern technology. There were no newspapers or magazines, so if you wanted to gossip to someone back then, you had to get on your horse or walk to your friend's house to chat. The tools and means to make a living were simple, but that didn't mean life was any simpler. The leaders mentioned in my poem were human; they had human struggles like we do now. Most of them had to contend with the monarchs of their time just to get God's point across. Slowly, the United States is becoming this way. As we trudge along through the year 2011 people become more ignorant on the subject of Christ and show the same indifference that the people of Noah's time showed just before the flood. In Luke 17:26 Jesus Himself stated, "When the Son of Man returns, the world will be like the people were in Noah's day. In those days before the flood, the people enjoyed banquets and parties and weddings right up to the time Noah entered his boat and the flood came and destroyed them all." The story does not end here. Jesus Christ will return, whether we like it or not.

God is still forming people into His own image so that they may preach to those who are still unaware or are aware but do not take the warnings seriously. Right now, people are marrying and giving in to marriage. There is nothing wrong with marriage, but now marriage is being used as a cover-up and disguise to condone immorality and minister to passion, which was contrary to what God ordained marriage to be. Marriage is supposed to be a holy communion between a man and a woman, but even God's name is taken off marriages now. If we want God to mold us into His image, we must first allow God to cut off the parts that are harmful and may lead us to destruction. In John 15:1, Jesus refers to Himself as the "true vine" and God as the "gardener." He says that God will cut off every branch that does not produce fruit and prunes the branches that do produce fruit so they will produce even more.

If God gave you ability that you have already started using for Him, continue to let Him fine-tune that into something powerful and potentially life-changing. Here's a personal testimony: I used to rap. I know some of you who know me well may look at this and say, "Yeah, right," but it's true. I did not release any CDs, but I do have a demo showing a performance done at the Attic. I was writing well—so well, in fact, that I started to think about going to the booth and dropping a couple verses. But God came and fine-tuned me so His presence can be shown much more through my writing. As a result, I converted to poetry, because I felt that with rap, the young people today would be clouded by the fancy lights, beats, and rhythm of the songs, and less attention would be given to the actual words. Trust me, I know. When I listened to secular music, most of the time, I was admiring the beat rather than the actual song. With that knowledge, I would prefer that my words speak and that God would mold future leaders through my words. Remember that the future is still yours; it's just not guaranteed to fall in your favor. Whenever you get a chance, pray for God to mold you—just like the potter molded his clay jar.

CHAPTER 6

Never Can Say Good-bye

I left my heart in NYC

As I walk down the Jamaica Coliseum, memories start to flow
looking at the places I used to go and people I used to know
As the music blared and people gathered in a festive air
I know that deep inside myself, I have to beware with care
be aware that the music doesn't take over me
to take heed of my own creed, to consider responsibility
of letting the music control and take hold of me
'cause if the music gets a grip, I know I won't leave
It has a spell on me, constricting me so hard I can't breathe
I begin to fall in love with this diverse community
I can't deny that I left my heart in New York City
I'm infatuated by the many familiar smells and sights
that have continued to draw me since my recent flight
The scene illuminates as birds landed in a slow glide
I walked with the company of a beautiful guide
A wise, friendly native who knew every turn and twist
Her laugh and friendship is among those I'll miss
Being in Queens, New York revitalized a feeling I'll never forget
although I regret seeing people who I haven't fully met
Streets are filled with hot dog and ice cream vendors
people of all personalities and color, of origin and genders
Being separated from the harmony of diversity leaves a dent
my back bent because my week is already spent
I refuse to vent, because I know I have to be content
But in my heart, I know that I belong in that harmony
Bring me back to my hometown of New York City.

Life in Queens, New York

Being a youth leader for a growing ministry such as the DIRT Crew has been an eye-opening and humbling experience. As the years passed, I watched the members of our youth group grow and develop in their relationships with Christ. I can't even begin to describe the awesome feeling I get when I see another youth member make the decision to receive Christ as their personal Savior, especially when that person is a young age. Teaching and preaching to adolescents ages twelve to seventeen taught me that these kids could be anywhere, but the fact that God has led them to His house, the rock that He called His church, is very encouraging. Even more encouraging is when they had questions about their walk and came to me for advice.

The DIRT Crew holds a retreat every summer, and I had the pleasure of serving as a leader at the camps. In the camp that took place in Dade County, Georgia in 2008, I was a group leader. On the last night at camp, we would huddle up in front of a campfire in the mountainside. All the campers would describe the leader who inspired them the most and who they most looked up too. One camper who was in his first year of camp said, "The most influential person in my life has been Marc, because he always helps me every day with my spiritual walk, and he helped me in my decision to give my life to Christ." When I heard that, I was deeply touched, and his words gave me a feeling of accomplishment. But I also felt a sense that I passed on knowledge and faith to a young boy—just as many leaders in the past has done for me. I will always be grateful to Brian Lee, Barry Dollar, and the rest of the Eastwood Baptist family for shaping me and honing my leadership skills. But my blueprint—the place where it all began—has always been in my hometown of Richmond Hill, New York in the borough of Queens. At Bethany French Baptist Church in Jamaica, Queens, I was raised and taught by many leaders and ministers. Through them, I was introduced to the gospel. Just like the camper at DIRT Camp, I was once a shy, confused boy. Through words and songs, I have learned many values and scripture applications. If not for the leaders in Bethany who were an inspiration to me and took me under their wings, I would not have been able to inspire and take other young people under my wing when the time came.

In the background information given in this book, I merely touched on a few points of my early life in New York, and I really didn't list any positives. In this chapter, you will learn that no matter how much I went through or what trials I faced as a kid or in my early teens, I still love New York. I love everyone I grew up with. I hold no ill will for those who gave me a hard time growing up; rather, I wish them the best, and I will continue to pray for them. During my early years in Queens, I didn't grow up with much—though since I was an only child for about seven and a half weeks, my parents did do their best to make sure I wasn't bored. I went to birthday parties, had sleepovers at friends' houses, and just chilled when I had the chance to. When my other two brothers were born, it created a little bit more strain and support. I'm thankful that they were born, but some privileges I had before their births were a little hard to come by. What was worse was that about 60 percent of my time was spent babysitting or watching my brothers whenever my parents left the house.

I touched on the schools I attended while I was in New York, and I have different views toward them. All had their positives and negatives. The first school I attended, St. Teresa of Avila, was good school. It was kind of stiff and structured, though. It felt like there were rules for everything. It seemed that I was always getting into trouble. To top it all off, it was a Catholic school, so we had to go to church for two days a week. If I had been a little bit older—about nine or ten—I would've been a bit more mature about it, but I was six. At that age, none of the chanting or rituals meant anything to me.

I then attended Public School 50. As you read earlier, my first year there was not so good. But the years that followed were not so bad. I still passed all my classes with good marks, and I had memorable field trips with them as well. The trip I remember was to a theater in Queens to see a presentation of *Hiawatha*, which was a play depicting a courageous Indian boy. In my middle school years, I attended Junior High School 217Q, and the first year there was rocky. Richmond Hill was a tough area. Overall, it's okay—if you mind your own—but if you walked down the wrong place or stuck your nose in someone's business, that may as well be your last day. I'm not trying to scare anybody or brag about it, but it's the truth. My old neighborhood had gangs running left and right—some dubbing themselves Bloods and Crips. But that was only the tip of the scale. There were more gangs in the area.). The worst thing was that you did not know who was or was not in it. My thought was that if a person didn't meddle with me and minded his own business, he would be all right. I even had a couple friends who associated with and were in gangs. If I walked home or walked to the corner to take a bus home, I would walk with a friend or a group of people, because I feared walking home alone. If I did walk home alone, I would always look behind my back, because I never knew. People are walking frequently in Queens, and a young boy could easily be a target. It's a habit that I couldn't shake—even when I came down to Georgia. Sometimes I had trouble trusting people, and during my young years, it showed. But 217Q also had good moments, and I feel like I shed a little bit of my outer shell there.

But the one place where I felt I could be myself was Bethany French Baptist Church. Yeah. That place was something else to me. From causing trouble as a kid with my good friend, Caleb, to growing up and joining the junior choir, there was always some adventure. There was always something going on—some type of drama—but it wasn't anything that the leaders could not squash. I won't remember *everybody,* but I will have to shout out some honorable mentions. My Sunday school teachers were great; Caleb's mother taught the class. She made the class lively and taught us different songs. I rarely ever saw her mad in class, although I did see her get mad when she yelled at Caleb, and even though I was at the scene of the crime too, I wouldn't get punished (unless my dad caught me). I want to thank Caleb's mother, Laura, for everything she did for me.

Medine Toussaint later got married and moved to Florida. She was probably the *best* teacher I had. She used to make us laugh with her jokes, but she always got the lesson across. Subsequently, she was also the youth choir director, along with another teacher I had, Brother John Parfait. The youth choir had it *going on* back then. The church also had a great step team, and a drama team as well. I was at the drama team at Eastwood Baptist (where I attend now), but it wasn't the same. The youth choir *loved* what they did. They loved serving God through music, step shows, and skits, and they were enthusiastic about it.

Another influential leader was Joel Desir. Brother Joel was the youth director for the kids my age, and he and my dad's friend, Jocelyn Augustin, started a youth program on Fridays from about 5:00 to 7:00 p.m. The program is now called Teenz for Christ, and in 2009, they celebrated their tenth anniversary. I had the pleasure of attending this celebration. With additional leaders headed by the youth president, Brother Maxime Yvinx, who was later succeeded by Brother Freddy Germain and Teddy Castor, the youth of Bethany were on point with messages, skits, and even a fair share of field trips.

My fondest memory of New York is the *food*—*m*an, the *food*. I ate everything under every nationality except Indian food. I had Chinese, Jamaican, Hispanic, and Italian dishes at least once a year, in addition to good old Haitian dishes I was accustomed to. The ice-cream trucks are symbolic in Queens. It's just not the same in Georgia. These ice cream and Italian ice vendors turned frozen dessert into an art form, and the desserts were quick, cheap, and delicious. The summers in New York were memorable, with trips to beaches, picnics at parks, and water gun fights with Super Soakers.

I loved winter as well. My boys and I always had snowball fights outside the school yard. We took trips to Manhattan to see the big tree at Rockefeller during Christmas. For the ladies who are reading this, if you love to shop, New York is a shopper's paradise—especially the malls in Manhattan and Broadway. A woman can lose herself shopping. Of course, being a boy, I *hated* shopping—especially shopping for clothes. My mother would drag me to Marshall's, Target, and many places down Jamaica Coliseum, which was a long street that stretched two or three blocks and had many department stores linked together with food chains. There would also be music blaring on loudspeakers, so it became a hangout spot.

When I returned to New York in 2009 to attend the tenth anniversary of the Teenz for Christ program, it seemed as if nothing has changed. Of course, people got older, and some of the stores that were around before I moved were no longer around, but the atmosphere was the same. I felt like I had never left, and I felt like I didn't *want* to leave. When I went to JFK Airport to leave for Atlanta, I had a sense of longing. Prior to that visit, I had not been to New York for six years, and I had not seen my friends for eight years. I got emotional when I came back to Georgia, and I wrote a poem to simply reflect on how much I love New York and how much it meant to me. But I also wrote the poem to reflect on the impact Bethany Baptist had on me. Every word of it is true and inspired by the Most High. I plan to come back to New York (God willing), but I will continue to grow and work for Him down here in Georgia, because for the first time in my life, I meant something to someone at the DIRT camp. I mean something to the youth group down at Eastwood.

One thing I will never do is forget where I came from—my Haitian background and my Queens roots. I often reflect back on Joseph in the Bible, who was sold by his brothers to Egypt. I bet there were moments when Joseph was homesick for his native land—when he was a slave to Potiphar, was jailed for a crime he didn't commit, or when he was the second-highest ruler in Egypt after he interpreted Pharaoh's dreams. His love for his homeland was displayed when after twenty years, Joseph, upon revealing himself to his brothers, allowed his brothers, his father, and his entire homeland to populate the land of Goshen. That action says a lot about Joseph's character. Even when his brothers did wrong, Joseph did not repay it with wrong.

Have you ever heard the saying, "Two wrongs don't make a right"? That saying is very true. We must repay anger with kindness. I have endured many things in New York, and I have done many things that I am not proud of in New York. But none of that matters, because when all has been said and done, New York is my home. Jamaica Ave. is my home. Even though I can't give a land to my friends and fellow brothers and sisters in Christ, I can give them what I have. I can still give moral support, financial support, or whatever else they need, because that's Christ in *me*. I'm not doing it to earn any points or for public approval. I'm showing my gratitude for the people who changed my life, changed my view, and were there for me when I needed someone to lean on. Bethany has shown me that I can lean and focus on Christ at all times. My heart will always belong to God, but a portion of it will stay behind in New York, where I took it all from.

CHAPTER 7

Stand Up

Not Here to Please Anybody

I ain't here to claim to be great or take your bait,
So try to concentrate as I set the record straight.
Y'all wonder why I don't walk with a swagger
My words do the walkin' so it don't even matter
So let me be brief, meek as I remain discreet
Those who attempt to oppose will soon admit defeat
I work and run my race at my own pace
As my God-given gift takes me to a unique place
There's no question among men when I pick up the pen
Until the piece is done; then I'm at it again.
I'm alone in my own time zone, trying to hone
what I say; it sends chills down your spine and bone
With my words, I attack the proud, lift the down
As I captivate the crowd with the talent found
My words will strike like a bolt of lightning
At times even my own writing's frightening
So those who despise, those who criticize
I'll pray that God opens your blind eyes
For those of you who choose to hate or interrogate
or regurgitate the soul food I put on your plate
Those of you who choose to spite what I write
or those of you who elect to fight what's right
and those who compel me to face my trial by fire
From the silent assassins to the open liars
Thank you for the drive and the motivation
For your strong negativity I reap stronger determination
I'm not gonna modify my style or be rearranged
For I am who I am, and will never change.

The Power of Faith

It's been almost eight years since I moved to Georgia, but I began to hit my stride. Upon graduating high school, I visited colleges around Georgia and Florida. I was involved in ministry, just practicing and working on my spoken word. More importantly, I was more confident than ever in my writing talents and abilities. I've worked three jobs already, and I made money for myself and the family. Everything started happening for me—one thing after another. Before I knew it, I was on another job hunt, and for almost four months, I was unemployed. My savings were dwindling.

Fortunately, while I was driving home from church one day, I heard on the radio that Ryla Teleservices, a call center founded by Mark Wilson, was hiring customer service agents. The moment I heard the radio ad, I raced home to apply online for a position and schedule an interview. The process took nearly a whole day. Ryla ran a background check, and I took drug screening tests. I had to fill out benefit applications and payroll papers. The whole thing was exhausting, but it was gratifying. I finally had a substantial job, and I was not going to pass up an opportunity to show them my best.

Training for Verizon Wireless customer service agents began in March of 2009, and the training class was *packed.*

There were people from different places, all of varying age, size, and qualifications. On the first day, when we had to introduce ourselves to the whole training class, I found out that some people were more than qualified. In fact, a few of them had already graduated college with their bachelor's degrees, and they were working on their master's degrees! I thought, *Wow, these people could have applied for better jobs than this.* But the reality was that at that time, Americans were experiencing negative effects from the recession caused by a massive loss of jobs. Newly elected president Barack Obama had his work cut out for him as he tried to stop the recession by trying to open up jobs for people and giving bonuses to employees who were underpaid.

So here we were, cooped up in this small training classroom. There were other training rooms, and in order to categorize the training sessions, the rooms were named after Georgia colleges. There was Georgia Southern, Kennesaw State, Mercer, University of Georgia, and Georgia Tech. I was in the Georgia Southern training room, and we made ourselves known as the Fresh Crew. The duration of the training was long—about seven weeks—and we had to learn all sorts of material needed for the position of CSR (customer service representative). We had training Monday through Friday from 7:30 a.m. to 3:30 or even 4:00 p.m., depending on the lesson. We had two breaks—one in the morning and one in the afternoon—highlighted by a one-hour lunch in the middle of the day. The trainer, Sharon Kellman, was a very intellectual, interactive trainer who would use examples and visuals to make the training sessions understandable and less boring. (It was still boring—at times, I found myself dozing off!) There were days— notably on Fridays—when we would take mini-breaks in the classrooms. During those mini-breaks, we would have an in-class talent show. Now many people in that class were talented, but a few people displayed their talents.

Word got around that I was a poet. I don't know how that started, because I only told a couple people about my skills in writing and reciting poetry. Then a couple friends urged me to go to Sharon and ask her to read my poem at a talent display. At first I refused, because I was not familiar with my surroundings, and this would be the first time I read my poem in a *workplace environment*. None of my coworkers at previous jobs knew I was a poet, and I wanted to keep it that way. But just to show my friends up, I went to Sharon, and she agreed to let me read a poem that I had just scribbled down that morning. The poem was called, "The Call of Confidence." I used a two-person dialogue in a poem for the first time. I created a scenario between a customer and a customer service agent, and the poem was nice. The poem had a rhythm to it. I suddenly felt more confident after that point, because after I finished, I received an accolade of claps and snaps from my peers. It was so good that people wanted me to read again at our next talent display.

The following week, I took the opportunity to read a poem that made people reflect on their spiritual lives. The poem was titled "Heaven," and in it I described God's kingdom and the beauty of it. This poem was also well taken, but I did have a couple skeptics. One man felt that I was too soft. He felt like I was a punk and couldn't stand up to anybody. I had enough bullies growing up. I didn't need another one, so I decided to squash all that drama before it started.

One Thursday, this guy spread a rumor that I was still a virgin and I don't know how to get down like everybody else. That was it. He crossed the line. I could take all the jokes he was throwing in my face, but once he went behind my back and started to spread things about my personal life, it was like a slap in the face. At first I was angered to the point that I wanted to resort to childish jabs and start saying things like "yo mama." We were all adults, and I had to act in an orderly manner. So then I decided that I was not going to embarrass him; I was just going to humble him. That night, with music blaring in my mp3 player and my mind focused on the task at hand, I took my poetry notebook and wrote a couple rough drafts. I fused the drafts into one poetic masterpiece—the poem you read above. It can be passed off as freestyle or a rap, but for the record, I'm just going to say that it was about using God's gift to humble someone. The best thing about it was that he wouldn't see it coming. It would catch him completely off guard.

The big day came, and I had my poem in my folder. I was ready to dish out something the class never seen before. The man was sitting there, talking his usual game, and I could hear the snickering and giggles behind me. Then the talent display was in full effect. Sharon called my name, and I took my customary breath before stepping up to the front of the room. Stares and anticipation followed me up to the stage, and I was ready. With my poem in hand, I didn't care about anyone else in the room— which was totally uncharacteristic of me. I stared directly at the guy and started blasting the poem at him. When I say blast, I mean, I *blasted* him. I let the brother have it. I read the piece very vigorously, raising my voice at the right moment and pausing at the times I wanted to so I could induce suspense. I stared right at *him* while I was reading it.

People's eyes followed my gaze to meet him, and they were astounded by how my rhymes hit him—line by line. It was the defining moment of that month. After I was done, I didn't get claps and snaps like I received with the other two poems. I received a standing O—not unlike the praise I received at the Attic. People gave me my props when I went back to my seat. The man I directed my poem to just sat there in complete shock—then he laughed it off. But I earned my respect that day. There was no denying the poem I read and the message. My talent, my gift, who I was, and how I lived my life were dedicated to the one and only Jesus Christ.

I don't have to prove myself to anybody. But if I have to defend God and His laws and statutes, I will stand up for Him and watch God consume any man's pride and doubt with His fire. The man who had mocked me stopped talking about me that day, and for the rest of the training, he and I were good friends. People started to give me their e-mail addresses. They wanted copies of the poem, because they liked it that much. God does not condone revenge, but there has to be a time when we have to stand up and make a statement for our salvation and defend the honor of Jesus Christ.

A great, classic example of making a statement with God's power can be found in 1 Kings 18. The prophet Elijah is in front of the people of Israel, challenging the 450 prophets of the idol Baal at Mount Carmel. Elijah gave the people a message from God, asking, "How long will you waver between two opinions? If the Lord is God, follow him; but if Baal is God, follow him" (1 Kings 18:21)(NIV). Then Elijah told the people that he and the prophets of Baal would erect two sacrificial offerings God and Baal, and whoever consumed the sacrifice with fire from heaven was the one true God. The people and the prophets agreed to this, and two bulls were sacrificed at an altar. The prophets of Baal called onto their god to consume the sacrifice, but their god was silent. Then they tried cutting themselves, thinking that human blood would persuade Baal to come and consume the sacrifice. Even Elijah started to taunt them, saying, "Maybe you need to shout louder! Perhaps he's in deep thought, or maybe he's sleeping and has to be awakened!"

Then Elijah said, "Come to me." He wanted everyone—even the prophets of Baal—to experience God's power. Elijah re-erected the altar, placed twelve stones to represent the twelve tribes of

Israel, had his sacrifice ready, and poured water down the trench that surrounded the offering. He then asked God to show Himself in front of the people so Israel would believe that God was the one true God. Then the fire from the Lord came down from heaven and consumed the sacrifice. When the people saw this, they fell to their knees and said, "The Lord—He is God!" Elijah had the false prophets of Baal sentenced to death that day.

Talk about making a statement. Standing up for God is definitely not for the weak-hearted. If you do not have faith that the Lord is God or that what you do or how you act represents Him until the very end, then there is no divine salvation from within, and God will not consume those around you until your spirit has been consumed by the Holy Spirit. I believe that God has a plan for me. I'm going to continue to follow Him at His word and will. God has a way to humble and silence all those who are proud and boastful, and He will be there to defend you when you wear His full armor.

CHAPTER 8

Gotta Get Off the Block

Keep on Writin'

Wake up in the mornin' 'round the time of nine
Knowin' that today meant goin' through another grind
Glare of that southern sun is so bright it's blindin'
But still gotta thank God that I see it shinin'
So I get up out of bed, my eyes still red
should I use Colgate? Nah, I'll use Crest instead
Walked outside to get me some fresh air
Dew from the grass wet my feet, but I didn't care
Later on, got ready for work the best way I could
Probably gonna be five minutes late, but it's all good
Put on my shirt and tie; trying to be quick as lightnin'
Then I hear a voice in me that says, "Keep on writin'."
I'm cruisin' in my Ford down the bumpy Cobb road
See a truck with a sign in the back that reads, "Wide load"
Then a Honda cut me off as I swerve by a curb
Man, these drivers get me on my last nerve.
So while this whole thing was still happenin'
Something in me says, "Don't sweat it; keep on writin'."
I arrive at work and I sit at my normal desk
I really gotta start cleanin', cause my station's a mess
Came home real early which was a bit surprisin'
I hear my inner voice which is still sayin', "Keep on writin'."
With my pen in hand, my pad staring at me, empty
I begin to work, slowly then steadily, then freely.

Keep On Writing

Fervently, my pen skates over the paper, looking for the right words to write. But the words refuse to go onto the paper. My mind's a jumbled mess. I can't get my head straight for this poem. The mound of crumpled paper behind me gets bigger than Mt. Fuji, and I'm wasting a bundle of time. I have the right tools; the right tune is playing in my head, transported through a pair of cheap headphones.

I was all alone in my room with the right mindset, but nothing was being written on that paper. I was suffering from the worst case of writer's block. There was nothing worse. I got frustrated and more worked up than ever. I'm not usually a guy who overreacts out of anger, but when I have nothing to write about, I get burned up inside. I knew that the devil was trying to attack me by reducing my words and written praises to God, but it was not enough to just know the devil's strategy. I had to fight it. I had to resist the urge to quit and keep going. When this poem was written, I was pretty much squeezed into a routine lifestyle. I would wake up in the morning and get all my morning activities done. Then I had to drive to work every day, and I just had to add that little bit in there about the truck. Most of the time, it wouldn't be trucks, but station wagons, punch buggies, Hondas, and vehicles that had drivers who did not happen to wake up yet! Thank God Ryla, the call center where I worked, was about ten minutes from my house.

Sometimes some events would happen that I would want to place on my mind so I could write about them later on. When I arrived at work, though, something else would come up. Our computers would have system issues, and we would have to wait for maintenance to come by and fix them. Other times, someone took my headset or sat at my cubicle, and as a result, I lost an hour of pay. Then when I actually got to work, I had to have patience to endure some customers who were complaining about their phone service and the outrageous balances on the bill. At the end of the day, the event or inspiration that I had initially planned to write about became pure vapor. I let the constant events of everyday life interfere with what I wanted to do. That's what would lead me back to my room with my pen, empty piece of paper, and absolutely nothing to write about.

The inspiration that led to write this poem was actually the story of the inspired men who wrote the Bible, especially those who wrote the Gospels when Jesus walked among men. These men were regular, hardworking individuals—just like we are. They had jobs, and I'm pretty sure that they always had distractions going to and from their jobs. But they did not let those distractions sway them from who they were following. The things that they witnessed from Christ day after day must have been amazing. Even when He spoke in parables, Jesus gave His disciples real-life examples of how His teachings impact the course of human spiritual life. I have seen amazing things—both great and terrible—happen in the twenty-first century. When I write, I think about future generations. I always have a vision of my kids and my grandkids reading the events I recorded—not just read it by paragraph or in "school form," as I like to call it, but reading it dynamically so they can learn through unique word use and rhyme schemes that will keep them aroused and interested.

When I read the Gospels in the New Testament, I feel like I'm reading perseverance. When I read the Gospels, I feel like I'm reading the stories of men who did not let something as annoying as writer's block get in the way of what they had to record. All the books of the Bible are inspired this way; I'm just using the Gospels as an example to prove my point. When my poems, books, and records are read and through my writings, people are motivated to read the Bible, I can't help but have feel like I did my job. Some people do certain jobs merely for the satisfaction of getting paid, but I don't do this for money. I love serving people, because this is what Jesus Christ did when He was on earth. And when He ascended into heaven, He gave us a commission to go and preach to others about Him. I can't let a little writer's block keep me from doing what I'm commissioned to do. No matter what I go through or how many people I interact with every day, I must keep writing for future generations.

CHAPTER 9

A Year of Struggle

2009

2009 was a time that brought forth great triumphs and heartache
A year that saw more struggle than anybody can ever take.
January found me out of the game without a penny in my name
Thoughts of being below standard started to infect my brain,
With nothing to gain, into February; the months transitioned
and I was still in the same position with nothing in my disposition
New opportunities to make a living began to open up in display
But this was not the opportunity I wanted to seize—not this way
As winter became spring, I thought of only one thing,
The chance to live till the decade and what '10 will bring.
The summer came around, but my circle of influence died down
As old friends and comrades I knew well began to leave town.
The economic woes of the nation continued to whip our backs like slaves
as more of the earth's population made early entrance into graves.
With hopes of entering an institute of higher education in the fall
The feeling of importance and gratitude began to conquer all
But I was appalled when my dreams were ground into the dust
The fact I must wait for my chance to succeed caused greater fuss
So the year 2009 found me on my desk doing what I do best,
Writing about the year's tests and letting God handle the rest
The year has been a year of pain for the nation and a year of isolation
The mission is to enter the new year with a completely new sensation
To make the year 2010 a year of my emergence and resurgence.

The Storms of 2009

"We can rejoice too, when we run into problems and trials, for we know that they are good for us-they help us learn to endure" This verse is found in the letter Paul wrote to the Romans in Romans 5:3(NLT). In reading this verse, I realize that if anyone knew about running into many problems and trials, it was the apostle Paul. This is a man who had been whipped, beaten, thrown in jail numerous times, and bitten by a snake—and here he was, still preaching and spreading the Word of God. How many of us can go through many trials and tribulations in our lives and still be encouraged by God's words and promises? This is the question that can test how real and grounded our faith in Christ is.

Every year of my life had its share of hardships and trials, but until now, I never felt truly tested until I lived through the year 2009. I chose this year in particular because 2009 was a very difficult year for me and my family, as well as for the US economy. As jobs were decreasing and more homes were being foreclosed, all I could do was pray for the nation and hope that President Barack Obama could make a change in his first term at the White House.

The previous poem actually followed a tough road I walked, dating back to the conclusion of 2008. In the fall of 2008, I was in my second full semester at Kennesaw State University in

Kennesaw, Georgia, and I had an average part-time job as an inventory clerk in a retail outlet store called Brandsmart USA. The pay was not bad at the time—$8.00 an hour—and the hours were from 9:00 a.m. to 1:00 p.m. I went to classes in the afternoon, and I still attended church and the Attic on Wednesday nights to help lead the DIRT Crew ministry. Then my world took a turn for the worse.

On September 28, Cobb County (which is the county Kennesaw, Acworth, and Marietta resided in) gave me a summons to serve jury duty in civil court for two to three months. While the jury duty experience was a learning experience, it was very time-consuming. I would have to be at the courthouse by 9:00 a.m., read, and decide on countless cases until 4:00 p.m. on Tuesdays and Thursdays. As a result, I missed classes and work, and my performance in both began to suffer. If you had to serve jury duty, the jobs would excuse you for working with the government, but I had a feeling that the Brandsmart supervisors didn't like the job I was doing anyway. I knew it would be a matter of time before I would be given the boot. I just did not expect it to be so early. The month of October came, and I was busy at work, counting the supplies the store had in stock. I used the faulty scan guns that were never replaced or fixed. Upon completion, I put the scan gun down and called in my counts to the supervisor. Unfortunately for me, the supervisor did not receive the counts I did, and even though I tried to explain to him that the scan guns were defective, I was fired. I had no job.

I continued to go to jury duty and attend classes every other day. The jury duty pay was minimal, and I was only paid $25 per *day*. In December, it finally ended—but so did my school semester. When my grades were released, I found out that I didn't perform up to standard, and I was placed on academic suspension for one semester. Now I had no school or job. From the end of December of 2008 to the month of February in 2009, I was basically languishing at home, unemployed and uninspired. I didn't realize right away that I was being tested until I had absolutely nothing.

Then God started to use me, and He knocked some sense into me. I couldn't just stay at home and do nothing. So 2009 came, and the United States was going through problems of its own—a struggling economy. While the United States was struggling to get back on its own feet, so was I. In February, I was finally hired by Ryla, which was a customer service call center. God has answered my prayer for a job. Things were moving a little, which was good. But it was not done yet. I still had to get back to school, and I was primed to do so in the summer of 2009. But the summer of 2009 came, and I find myself wasting time. Satan was using my worst enemy—procrastination—and he used it effectively. Before I knew it, summer arrived, and I was still working like a mindless drone, not pursuing much of anything. My life had gotten so routine by now that even my personal relationship with Christ was failing.

I wanted to go back to school in the summer. I thought I was ready at the time, but I wasn't. I got ready for fall of 2009. During the summer, my ego took another hit when I heard about the deaths of Farrah Fawcett and Michael Jackson—on the *same day!* I was most hit by the death of the King of Pop. As a kid, I used to imitate his moves, watch his videos, and wear all hats fedora-style. Back in New York, Michael was the man, and if you said that you didn't know him or you didn't like him—well, it was nice knowing you. I was at the Ryla Cafeteria when I heard about Michael Jackson's death on the news. Everyone was sending text messages like crazy after it happened. I only hope that Michael Jackson saw the truth and accepted Jesus as his Savior, because though it may not be looking to good for him in eternal life if he didn't, I would hate to think of what would happen if the angel holding that Book of Life that has the names of the saved written in there shook his head at Michael. I mean no disrespect whatsoever, because Michael did great things here, but our earthly works are meaningless if Christ isn't behind them.

Just when I think I'm ready to go back to school in the fall, I can't, because I missed the registration date. I could not believe it. I missed out *again*. I had missed a whole year of school, and I thought I was going to be at Ryla till the day I died. It wasn't that I didn't like Ryla, but it does get hectic at times, and I didn't want to spend the rest of my life there. I just did not see myself staying there, because I simply wasn't happy with it. I was not *satisfied* with it. But the things I went through in 2009 strengthened me spiritually in 2010.

Another thing I dealt with was the mild emotional rift that I experienced with Brian Lee and the DIRT Crew. Since I had a new work schedule, I was not able to attend meetings regularly, and I told Brian about my work schedule. However, I wasn't the only one not attending. The Crew's numbers were dwindling fast, and the reason wasn't just because kids were growing. Kids were just not motivated to come to church anymore, and the Eastwood Baptist youth group was hit hard with non-attendance. This may have spurned Brian to post comments on my Facebook page, asking me when I was ready to get back in the game. I know now he meant well, but back then, I was insulted, because he was not respecting my schedule. It showed that he did not listen when I said I was not able to attend at the moment. I took it to mean that he cared about the ministry more than me as an individual, and it hurt.

Then a leader of the DIRT Crew and a friend, was married that same summer. Since he considered me a cousin of his, he didn't invite me to the wedding. Everyone else in the DIRT Crew (including Brian) attended, and I felt left out. Emotionally, I felt used. The double guilt I felt for not going back to school made me doubt my existence. Why was I even here? I didn't consider suicide before, but I sure contemplated on it at that time—that's how bad my depression was.

When I look back on it now, I'm happy that I didn't go through with it, because there is so much more that I could provide for God's children. God kept me alive for this purpose. 2009 may have been hard, but I knew it wouldn't get any easier. I had to keep close to God.

CHAPTER 10

The Winds of Change

Transition

As if I was in a sixth sense, I could feel His presence,
His words urging me to begin mirroring His eminence.
Inexperienced, inept, and incapable of fulfilling my destiny
There's nothing more than the heart that beats within me.
No bravery, no courage or strength that can be distinguished
Feeling as though the fruits of my labor would be extinguished
Have any of you ever felt that were constantly talked down to
that you once felt like a piece of broken glass people see through?
To work endlessly while trying to pick up shreds of your dignity
in an effort to impress the success for what seems an infinity?
I stand outside the fence, waiting one day for my comeuppance,
while the rest of the world shrugs and displays no repentance
I've waited for my chance when I can say, "I've been there"
when the rest of society dared, stared, and even glared.
Here's the chance to show the world that I have grown,
with the ability to take control of my life and be well known,
but to also be remembered as an individual who was meek
who kept his head up even though his future seemed bleak
To be a follower no longer but to be followed by the younger,
To quench their thirst for knowledge and feed their hunger
I want to be an agent for the Most High, to serve and commission,
'cause my mission is to complete my physical and spiritual transition
No longer a boy, but a man, ready to serve at His command
To be the one to lead my people into the Promised Land.

Changing for the Best

As I waited for the year 2009 to end and the year 2010 to begin, I reflected back on my recent struggles. I prayed for God to change the way things were. I also prayed that the new year would bring new blessings and that I would be used by God for a greater purpose as long as I was here on Earth. Finally, it was 2010.

At the time of a new year, people usually make New Year's resolutions and renew any commitments they failed to keep a year ago. In the meantime, the only commitment I was interested in renewing was my commitment to my relationship with Christ. I also had a thirst to be a leader wherever I was needed and to grow spiritually and physically. Five days into the new year, I wrote the previous poem after looking at some old pictures stored in a box at the house. The first thing I noticed was that as an adolescent, I was *extremely skinny*. During the years that I have been away from New York, I did not just grow taller, but I seemed to fill out more. I had more muscle, bigger hands, and of course, a bigger appetite! But I can't help that, because guys love to eat! I remember as a child, my mother always tried to fill up my plate so I would be fully fed. But I always refused, and when she did pile food on my plate, I usually did not finish the food. Now I was ravenous, and I ate whatever was placed in front of me that was edible.

The year 2010 also marked the year that I felt I was fully experienced in being a youth leader. I had been with the DIRT Crew for what seemed like ages, and I strived to have a youth group formed in the small Haitian church my family and I currently attend—First Haitian Baptist Church of Jonesboro. In the process of writing my poem, I thought back to when I first started preaching in front of the DIRT Crew. I remember how nervous I was and how I wanted everyone to like me and respect what I had to bring to them. The microphone quivered in my hand. I was too nervous to move around the stage. My timid voice read from the Bible while I anxiously looked at my notes to make sure I said everything. It was a tough process—one that I seemed I would never get over. But all that is over. Throughout the years, I learned that no matter how well you preach or spread the Word of God, all you can do is plant the seeds into people's hearts. We cannot force people to listen and adhere to the Bible and its teachings. But we can persuade and use God's word as proof and reproof of the Gospel. This is where I found most of my success.

In my trip back to New York in August of 2009, I will never forget the reaction of my friends when they saw how much I grew and how much I'd changed physically. In this poem, I strive to let people know that my change is much more than just physical. I wanted people to see that I grew in the Word and the knowledge of Christ as much as I wanted them to see that I was no longer the puny, skinny boy anybody could pick on. I don't want to be cocky, because when I say I wanted to prove that I have transitioned from boy to man, I don't want to be overconfident and say that I look or speak better than anybody. In truth, I am no better than anybody else, because I am also a sinner, and I need the grace of Jesus Christ as long as I am here and alive. All I wanted to do was send a statement to everyone who thought that a short-who-later-gets-tall-lanky-and-skinny-Marc was not going to amount to anything. I wanted to let people know that I could no longer be trampled on or overlooked, because those days were over.

When I was in New York, I did experience moments where people thought I was still the little, shy boy who grew up among them and did not contribute much. I felt discouraged. Then again, what doesn't hurt me makes me stronger, so I used the skepticism in my poetry and tried to balance power and humility. This poem also marked the beginning of a new path for me. The new path was this: No longer would I follow men or let men other than God decide the way I live my life and the way I serve Him. I would still obey my parents and respect my elders, because the Bible has asked us to do so, but I would no longer be a mindless follower of peers whose only goal in life was to distract me and turn me away from my walk with Christ. I would take advice, and I would listen, but I would not be anybody's robot who could be programmed to do whatever anyone told it to do. No more. I've been around long enough to know that no matter who you choose to follow or imitate in life, it will always separate into two roads. One road may lead to goodness and worldly riches. The other road may lead to destruction and possibly imprisonment or death. I choose to follow *neither*. I intend only to follow the word of God—and that's it. There are no variables, and there is no doubt in my mind about it. Atheists can no longer sway me with all that talk about how there can be no God and we are just living in this world to make a living and die. I will just tune them out now, so it won't work.

The theory of evolution used to shake my faith. But the theory of human evolution is not only unfounded, but also ridiculous. There was known to be a "missing link" that connects human to apes. But in reality, there is no missing link. One theoretical character named Lucy, who is supposed to be a mix between chimps and humans, is actually no more than a skeleton of a three-foot chimpanzee. The most complex character, Neanderthal Man, whose skull was found in France, was actually a skeleton of a man who suffered from arthritis. Further studies were done to come up with the conclusions that I record in this book.

While the transition from ape to man is false, my transition from boy to man is pretty much reality. After taking unneeded and unwanted advice that was not going to benefit me at any time, I felt that enough was enough. To sum it all up, I wrote the poem to show people that transition is possible and that I had evolved physically and spiritually, by the grace of God. As a result, things are picking up for me. I'm back in school with a renewed mind, I'm still working part-time at Ryla, and I am more involved in the ministry now than ever before. God has allowed me to preach three messages at Jonesboro, and I can sense that the power of God is working in people after they hear a great message that is not coming out of a boy's mouth—it is coming out of one of the Lord's men.

I have transitioned into a better person. Everyone has the same opportunity to change for the better and help others transition into better people. I remember that after I completed the poem, I drove to work, and I heard a song by gospel artist Marvin Sapp. The song basically describes how God saw the best in us when everyone else around could only see the worst. I felt that God wanted me to hear the song at that time because He knew how far I'd come, and He knows how far I have to go. Back in the 1990s and at the start of the millennium, everyone saw a skinny kid who was shy and could never muster up the strength to do anything in this life. But God saw a good poet and a great teacher. God sees my heart, and He knows my heart and soul better than me. When we come to the realization that God knows us better than ourselves and we can always be better than who we are, then we will transition to the same plateau of spiritualism and understanding.

PART 3

Let Me Encourage You

"But encourage one another daily, as long as it is called Today, so that none of you may be hardened by sin's deceitfulness"

(Hebrews 3:13)(NIV).

CHAPTER 11

The Kiss of Death

Cold as Ice

Our world's dominated by cold; it torments the young and old
We gather up in tight packs like sheep in the fold.
Ice slices through the air like blades, the sun fades,
Men wrapped up in scarves, maids tightening their braids
People made to conversate, but their teeth clatter and chatter
They rush to get home, but dwelling doesn't even matter
The cold creeps in as if a burglar in the dead of night
We don't move for fright, and help seems out of sight.
The cold moves boldly where the elderly sit, the lamp lit,
The tempest acts as he reacts as if he were bit,
His heart freezes within, he keels over in a dead faint
The cold leaves a trail as bleak as black paint.
It moves over to the young and helpless one
As he sleeps and dreams of the elusive sun.
The son is unaware as the cold settles and stares
It remains silent to prevent waking those upstairs
It moves very subtly, light as a bubble to the child
So lethal, yet so calm; so wild, yet very mild
The cold freezes the child from the very soul
It froze old Albert, and now it froze little Cole.
The tempest moves up to the second level
As if the driver of it was the devil.
It makes its way to the second son's room
locking the door, sealing his doom, but soon
The window opens and the savior comes in
Warmth accompanies Him with judgment of Cold's sin
In one quick motion so swift, the cold began to lift
As the savior shines through every roof and rift.
Don't shake and don't shiver, because the warmth delivers.

When Death Comes Knocking

I'm not going to lie about it. Death is not one of my favorite subjects to talk about. The fact that ten out of ten people die—that someday I am going to die—does not give me comfort at all. But death was the main subject of this poem, and the cold I mentioned describes how unpredictable and subtle death can be. Anyone can be the next one to go at any time. This is undoubtedly the darkest chapter you will read—but just like every chapter I've written, there is always hope and deliverance through the words of my book and through the Word of God.

When I was a child, I did not really understand death until I went to my first funeral around age eight or nine. One of the church members in Bethany had just passed away, and my parents attended her funeral. It gave me shivers when I saw the lifeless corpse lying there in the casket, unaware and unmoving. I don't think I'd ever walked so fast to my seat in church until I saw the body. It freaked me out, and I wanted to get out of there quickly. Before I really understood the meaning of death and the significance of death, I asked myself a few questions—why was death ever allowed? Does death hurt? When you leave this world—when you, as they say, "bite the dust"—is there any pain involved?

It's a good thing God sent His Word to answer all those questions. By reading Genesis 3, we see that death was actually a sentence imposed by God onto mankind for our disobedience to Him when Adam and Eve ate the fruit. Yes, I said *our disobedience.* Some people I have spoken to thought that they didn't deserve death and that they would've done anything to avoid it. But let me be the first to tell you that not one of us living in today's world would have resisted the temptation to eat the fruit that hung from that tree. We get distracted and tempted by *man-made* things every day, and we let variables such as money run our lives, time after time. Adam and Eve were living in *paradise,* where they were surrounded by God's natural beauty—no electronics, no money, no type of trade system—it was only them and God, and of course, the tempter, Satan.

Satan used stealth sloth and flattery to trick Eve into eating the fruit. If there is one thing that is considered human weakness, it is the fact that we can be influenced to believe the possibility of higher power is attainable. When Satan told Eve that eating the fruit would allow her to become like God Himself, knowing everything good and evil, Eve imagined herself being at the same level as God. Imagine being the ruler of everything, with unlimited power and the ability to discern between good and evil—all from eating this little fruit that hung from a seemingly harmless tree. It would have been enough to tempt the whole modern world. What's worse is that Satan can disguise himself as an angel of light and beguile us into believing that not everything we indulge in is bad.

Eve ate the fruit, and when Adam came by, she gave him the fruit as well. Then both of their eyes were opened, as Satan said—but their eyes were not open to higher rule, power, or omnipotence. Instead, their eyes were open to the truth and harsh reality of what they have just done. Both of them realized they were naked, and they sewed fig leaves to cover themselves out of shame. The world all of a sudden got cold to them, because they ate the fruit which was forbidden. When God came and asked them, "Where are you?" Adam replied, "I heard you, so I hid. I was afraid, because I was naked." God then asked who it was that told them they were naked. Both Adam and Eve confessed that they ate the fruit—but not before playing the blame game, where they pointed fingers at each other. Adam blamed Eve for giving him the fruit. Eve blamed the serpent for tricking her. Regardless of who influenced whom, all parties involved were punished.

Because of what Satan did, the serpent—known as a snake or reptile—was to be the most singled out and despised creature in the forest. Before that, it was a beautiful creature, respected by man and nature alike. But after this sin, the beauty was stripped from the serpent, and now the snake spends its time groveling and slithering on the ground. Eve's punishment was that childbirth was going to be painful and that she had to serve her husband. Women nowadays may not like the idea of being servants to their husbands, but the Word of God is written (Genesis 3:16). Sorry, ladies, I don't make the rules; I just pass it on from the King of Kings Himself. Adam probably had the bitterest pill to swallow. He was sentenced to forever work hard to support his family and struggle to make a living from his job. Then God said the statement that answered my question: "For you were made from dust and to the dust you will return."(Genesis 3:19)(NIV) Thus was the sentence of death passed onto mankind.

Adam's breath must have seized up within him once the judgment was passed. It's never easy to find out that we are destined to die one day. God gave us the first example of sacrifice when he covered Adam and Eve with animal skins. Ladies, if you ever want to know who wore the first fur coat in history, it was probably Eve! There was no red carpet, paparazzi, or anything to record that, but she definitely wore that mink coat! Getting back to the point, death was a sentence pronounced on us. We cannot avoid it, but we can control what happens *after* we die. A man named Jesus came down and defeated the power of death by dying on the cross for us. Just as God gave Adam and Eve clothing from animal skin to cover their nakedness and shame, God gave us a Savior in Jesus Christ to cover our sin and our spiritual nakedness with the blood he shed on the cross. Jesus is the warmth that is described in the poem.

Satan loves despair and hopelessness; he feeds on fear and relishes the power of doubt. The more we doubt God's word, the more cold and uncertain our futures get. If we don't stand together to fight this cold, the devil will have us so frostbitten with his evil desires that it will be too late. Do not let it be too late for you. Take the initiative and trust Jesus as Lord and Savior. Remember, there is no pressure—just love and encouragement from me and the Savior. The world is a cold place because it doesn't like us. You can see people one day, and then the next day, you don't hear from them again, or they die unexpectedly.

I had a co-worker at Ryla who was a good friend of mine. We would talk and joke around whenever we had the chance, and she was a nice woman. There couldn't be anyone nicer. On Thursday night, since she left before me, she told me, "Good-bye, I'll see you tomorrow." I never saw her alive again. The next day, on Friday, the supervisors and managers came up and called our customer service team into a small room. My friend had been in a fatal car accident, and she passed away. It's so amazing and yet devastating how quickly the breath of life can be taken away—in a heartbeat. We always make plans for everything, and we have an agenda for certain things—but we never plan on dying. The possibility that you can die within the next minute has never crossed your mind.

Death crosses my mind every day—but that's all it does; it crosses. It doesn't linger on my mind. My encouragement is to not allow death to hold the primary seat in your heart or mind. Rather, think about life. Think about this life and the next. Wake up every morning thankful that you lived to breathe another day and you get to enjoy life once more. Don't let a negative action be the last action that you perform on earth. Do something encouraging for others, and warm other people's hearts as God has warmed ours.

CHAPTER 12

Beauty's Only Skin Deep

Diamond in the Rough

You live your life with a burden of past regret
You won't let yourself move on or try to forget
You're leveled, because people think you're no good
"She's from the ghetto, so she must be straight 'hood."
You look in the mirror at your hair and count your split ends
You start to despise because you think you got no real friends
You try to do what's expected of you—what seems right
in a long, endless mind tunnel with a dimming light
As you stare into the glass, you hate what stares back
You develop a knack for seeking what you lack
The more you think, the more you blink
The more of the world's lies you continue to drink
You look at your room floor and see a magazine
You don't resemble the cover girl from Seventeen
She poses with her lean press-on body in a firm stance
You're in a trance as your eyes swivel and dance
This is your goal; this is your grand achievement
But follow this road; it will lead you to bereavement
You'll feel hollow and empty on the inside
Your access to self confidence will be fatally denied
Put down the magazine and stare at the mirror once more
This time, stare with a different perspective than before
Adore what you see without further deception
Be the driver in your life without opposing direction
Don't alter the way you look, for it's more than enough
No matter what people say, I still see a diamond in the rough
You are unique and beautiful, no matter who you are
You are fearfully and wonderfully made by far.

It's Not What's on the Outside

The most tumultuous years in an individual's life are probably their high school years. Many people may disagree with me on this one, but there are others who share my point of view. High school years are the years that groups and cliques are introduced, and girls are introduced into the world of plastic surgery and excessive makeup. Guys are taller, more athletic, and vainer than they ever had been when they were younger. The schoolwork, of course, gets harder, as plain addition and subtraction evolve into Euclidean geometry, algebra, and trigonometry (yikes!). Those who are talented enough to make it past those courses take calculus classes. Thank God I only stopped after trigonometry!

While some in high school begin to climb to their physical peak, there are also those who struggle internally. The worst part is that due to the fear of being ostracized by their fellow peers, they hide their internal struggles. What hurts me the most is seeing youth who have the potential to do so many things in life throw it away because they are trying to fit into a crowd. Imagine being blessed with a gift from God, but standing and continuing to be swayed by a group of posers. The way you look is the most important thing in high school. Let's face it—if you don't dress well and you don't smell good, chances are that you're not going to have a date for Friday night! Hygiene is important, but in high school, people would classify you by what brand of deodorant you wore or what type of sneakers you had.

The inspiration for this poem is what I saw throughout both middle school and high school, especially with the young women who I grew up with and associated with. I remember when I was in the tenth grade,I had a friend who was really friendly and nice. She did not look like any of the prima donnas who walked around the school. Then when I came back the following year for my junior year, I saw her again, and my jaw dropped. She must've dropped three or four dress sizes, and she looked a little hollow. She also went overboard on the makeup. To this day, I don't know who she was trying to impress that year—one particular guy, or the half the eleventh-grade male population. One thing was certain—she was not the same. Her attitude changed; her personality changed. It was like taking a step into the twilight zone.

When we change or alter who we are, it changes us inside. Now that we look the way the world wants us to look, we work so much harder to keep that image. We no longer thank the God who orchestrated our creation from the very beginning. We tend to forget that God has created us in His image, and that when He created us, He did not make any mistakes. In Psalm 139:14, David writes, "I praise you because I am fearfully and wonderfully made" (NIV). Remember, this is coming from the man who was dancing and jumping up and down for the glory of God—purely for the fact that He loved God so much. He did not care how that made him look. Even his wives rebuked him for dancing for what seemed like no reason. But there was a reason. There is still a reason to dance for God today. You're still alive. God has given you the opportunity to breathe fresh air once more. If you can still eat and digest food, that is another reason to thank God. If you can walk, that's another reason to thank God. It's about giving God all the praise, no matter who you are or how you look.

People everywhere go through extreme diet regiments, hoping to get thinner. People sometimes take it a little too far. Eating disorders plague the United States, and it's sad to think about another woman who becomes a statistic because her "dream diet" ends up being nothing more than a nightmare. Binging and purging is also unhealthy. When a person does this, the stomach is tempted with food in its system for only a limited time before it disappears right out of the mouth and into the bathroom sink. It is just sad. I blame the media for the health issues women and men face today. Thank God it's decreasing now—but about three to four years ago (maybe longer), Hollywood stressed the point that if you were not petite, were not thin in stature, and did not have a pretty face, you would not be accepted in society. It's a little harsh, but it's true.

Growing up, I must have seen about a thousand Slim-Fast commercials on TV. When the commercials showed the before and after pictures, I was thrown into a state of skepticism. Would a person really look like that after drinking a tasteless, rancid shake for two weeks? Trust me, I have tasted Slim-Fast before, and it was the most revolting thing I drank in my life (other than V8). It is important to stay in shape and continue to exercise and eat healthy foods. But it is not good to take the value of staying in shape to an obsessive-compulsive level where you are too self-conscious of the way you look and you have to change every little thing about yourself, including the diet you live on.

Another reason I wrote this poem was because I realized that guys (and I am not speaking for all guys—just the ones who are guilty of this) tend to classify women based on their background and the way they talk. If we see a girl walking down the block and she is wearing clothes that are showing more than what's necessary, we automatically think that she's a fast girl, and we label her as a hooker. I grew up listening to guys call girls names, and it angered me. Are they not human like guys? Don't they have feelings like guys do?

I've actually witnessed the gospel to girls who were self-professed prostitutes. Most of the time, money drives them to do what they do. They don't like their jobs, but they have to make a living to support their families. These women just need prayer, and they need God to give them something better so they can not only make others feel good, but they will benefit from what they do as well.

In my Ryla training class, there was a woman who had a four-year-old son, and she was judged almost immediately as "too hood" for the way she talked and dressed. But I got to know this lady better, and she was one of the most intellectual ladies I've met. She had also just rededicated her life to Christ, so she was a new Christian. It was hard for her to control her language at times. She was also a singer and a songwriter, and she had dreams of singing and owning her own label. Sometimes during our breaks, she wrote lyrics. She gave them to me and asked me what I thought of them. I saw her talent, and if there were any ideas about rhythm or word improvement I could provide, I would assist her in that aspect. Jesus sees her for who she truly is, so we have to see her talent. I know that if she continues to develop her relationship with Christ, she will go places only other people can imagine.

Through my coworker and friend, I have learned that we have to appreciate all shapes, sizes, and colors, because people may have much more to bring to the table in terms of their natural abilites. If we can love people who don't have high self-esteem or are feeling self-conscious about themselves, they can learn to love themselves and regard themselves as unique people who have something to give to the world—a talent that is so rare we can search the ends of the earth for it and only find a few of. As Jesus' parable of the lost sheep teaches us, the shepherd would go to extreme measures to locate the lost sheep. Jesus is willing to go to extreme measures to find us, because we are His diamonds in the rough. Do we want to be found for who we are?

CHAPTER 13

Ain't Too Proud to Beg

The Beggar's Story

A beggar shakes his cup as he walks down the street
hoping to get some money for some food to eat
His hat is ripped and his shoes are worn
His everyday clothes are tattered and torn
This isn't the way the beggar started.
When he was sixteen, his family and friends departed
forsaking him as if he was deaf and retarded
leaving him to this mess which causes him distress
without a wife or a loved one to touch or caress
His money cup is his only gift from the Divine
his only gold mine, his only link and lifeline
Even if he possesses no riches, he still has his cup
He still hopes against all hope that his life will pick up
As I walk by, he waves and shakes his survival link
Tears well up in his eyes, then he suddenly blinks
From that moment, I understand what I should do
I gave up my excessive wealth and say, "This is for you."
For I respect the struggle he makes day by day
Every time he felt delayed, he never doubted that God makes a way
I think of myself as a beggar from time to time
Poetry is my cup, and my words through God are my lifeline
My words may be plain, my legacy short-lived
But life lessons through writing are all I can give
Don't take your life for granted, for it's just a loan
Don't complain about what you have; don't moan or groan
Because the beggar's story may as well be your own.

Learning from the Beggar

The sun rises, and its bright rays hit your face immediately. You wake up from the bench that you slept on and roll up the newspaper that you used to cover yourself. You'll need it for tonight. You fix and adjust the collar on the shirt that you've been wearing for about eight or nine months. You put on your shoes that are two or three sizes too small for you; the soles are wearing out. With the pocket change you have, you go to the nearby Waffle House to grab some breakfast. At 10:00 a.m., you have to be out in the street to collect some money to make through the day.

From 10:00 a.m. to about 6:00 p.m., you stand on the side of the busy street and shake your cup, hoping a few kind people will bless you with some money. This is the only way you can make money now, and you need this more than anything. If you do not get enough, you will be forced to go eat at the shelter. You don't want to do that because of the horrible, stuffy conditions at the shelter. You'd rather make a living of your own. Every day is a struggle for you. You don't have any family to turn to, because all your family members have forsaken you. You keep walking, because in certain areas, loitering is prohibited, and if you stand somewhere for longer than thirty minutes, the police will get suspicious.

You've heard your share of insults in your lifetime, but the worst insult has got to be, "When are you gonna get a job, you bum?" It's not like you haven't tried, but no one has accepted you, and the house you once lived in was foreclosed because you could no longer afford to pay for it. The world can be so cruel—but at the same time, you have to keep on living. You have to try to get back on your feet. Sometimes you don't know if you can keep going.

Can you imagine living like that? Can you imagine scraping through life every day just to stay alive, eat, and continue to try to find a job to fulfill your life? I've been blessed with a loving family, a warm house to live in, and food on the table every day, but I've often thought about what it would be like if I had nothing. I've always visualized not succeeding and being in the streets, begging just to survive. I would have people look at me, feeling sorry for me but also being disgusted by me because I dressed differently, was unkempt, and was desperate for company and compassion. It was this vision that led me to write the poem that began the chapter.

In both New York and Atlanta, I have seen people who were struggling financially. Rough times have forced these people to the streets, where they are forced to live out of a shopping cart. In my old apartment in Richmond Hill, New York, there was one guy who stayed in the first floor of our apartment. He had a job, and he was a guy who was respected by everyone who lived in our apartment. Things were looking up for him. Then, without warning, his life took a turn for the worse. He lost his job, so it became a challenge just for him to pay rent. I saw the stress build in his face as he tried to look for jobs to keep up his payments. One day, I was walking home from school, and I saw him at the corner of the freeway with a cup in his hand. I couldn't believe that was the same guy who was living in my apartment. At that moment, I realized how cruel life was. If you don't land on your feet in certain situations, this life is going to swallow you whole.

Another experience I had was when I preached at the Atlanta Union Mission in downtown Atlanta. The Atlanta Union Mission was a Christian-based shelter, but it was much more than just a shelter. The Atlanta Union Mission also had daycare for women to put their children in while they worked. The mission also helped the men who resided there find jobs to support them and their families. Brian Lee and Chris Galloway were members of the Union Mission, and they took the DIRT Crew there every year for mission projects. The DIRT Crew would serve the people food, give them book bags and school supplies, and witness the gospel to them. Prior to that time, I had never preached outside the doors of Eastwood Baptist youth, and I was nervous. But God spoke through me that day, and I believe the Spirit moved some people to the point that they accepted Christ as their Lord and Savior. It was a satisfying and fulfilling experience, and I hope I helped people rekindle their faith in God. I hope the people believe that God will see them through their situations.

I also thought that if more people saw what was happening in their own city—if they saw the reality of being on the downside of life—more people would help. I felt the media had to play an important role in showing the reality of homelessness and how much support, prayer, and love our brothers and sisters need. I remember seeing a movie that did a good job of portraying this. *The Pursuit of Happiness,* featuring Will Smith, was a feel-good movie about a man who was smart, intellectual, and wise about business, but due to unfortunate financial situations, he found himself struggling. His home was foreclosed, his wife left him, and he was driven to the street. The saddest scene was when he took his son to the bathroom and they both slept in the public bathroom. I don't think the son had any idea they were homeless, but he trusted that his father was going to make something happen. Will Smith's character was so embarrassed and saddened by his situation that when someone attempted to open the door to use the restroom, he kept the door shut so that no one would see him and his son laying there. I don't think there has ever been a scene in a movie that brought tears to my eyes after that.

What we need to realize is that the homeless does not need money or financial stability. Money cannot buy happiness. But the love of God can get you happiness and joy. All that people need right now is God's love and mercy. Let's take a passage in Acts 3. Peter and John were on their way to the temple to take part in a 3:00 service. When they approached the temple, they saw a man who was lame from birth. He was begging for money in front of the gate called Beautiful. When Peter and John appeared, he was going to ask them for money, and Peter said, "Look at us!" The man looked up, expecting a gift, but Peter said, "I don't have any money for you. But I'll give you what I have. In the name of Jesus Christ of Nazareth, get up and walk."(Acts 3:6)(NIV) Immediately, the beggar's ankle and leg bones received strength. He began to walk, and then he leapt for joy, praising God. The beggar went in the temple with Peter and John. When the people heard him celebrating, they were amazed and could not believe that this man was the same man who was disabled at the gate earlier begging for money.

Peter and John show us that people who are struggling to make ends meet do not need money alone. Money can help you get just about everything in life, but money will never satisfy you. Only the love shown through the power of God in faith can give you the fulfillment and happiness you long for. Let the story of the beggar speak to your heart today. See his example—how pleased he was to know that he had someone who loved him. He has Someone who will continue to love him until the end of time.

CHAPTER 14

Life in the 'Hood

Pray for Better Days

My brutha, living this life is much more than work and play
Just listen to this tale of Michelle and Charles Day.
Michelle Day laid there on the floor in deep dismay
in complete disarray, holding on false hope that things would be okay

She laid there in silence, not knowing what to do
Her father was in the hospice and the rent was six months overdue
At the threshold of eviction, she was overwhelmed by conviction
Not wanting her husband to know of her recent condition

At 2:00 a.m. Charles Day made his way to the living room
carrying liquor as the acrid smell of alcohol loomed
With one greedy swig, he immediately quenched his thirst
Between his addiction and monetary situation, what was worse?

He cursed everything from his home to his job
where his paycheck was so meager he was forced to rob
keeping his .357 magnum strapped to his waist
he wasted no time to plunder, steal—even kill in haste

His dependent wife continued to resist, but he continued to insist
His lifestyle consisted of satisfying himself in drunk, euphoric bliss
But no matter how much he stole, he was still in debt
His wife, forced to be accomplice, broke down and wept

What's left of the modern man and the American Dream,
When life gives that cold shoulder, where else do we lean
Michelle Day will have to learn to live life the hard way
Remember, my brutha, when you pray, pray for better Days

A Brighter Day

Living a city life doesn't exactly mean living in a land of opportunity. In fact, there was little to no chance at all for black people to be really successful in the city. To say that you wanted to grow to make money and gain fame was almost a dream in my neighborhood. Of course, a few people from Queens made it big. As a kid, I couldn't help but look at those people with a sense of admiration. I think about hip-hop artists such as LL Cool J and 50 Cent. These guys are two individuals who beat the system and achieved their goals.

One of the biggest success stories, however, is the story of Christopher Wallace—or Notorious BIG, as he was known by fans everywhere. His childhood was often marred by a father who neglected him, the introduction into a world of hustling and selling drugs down the block, and time spent in prison. His big break came when he was discovered freestyling (rapping without written lyrics) on one of the streets he sold drugs on. After he was discovered, he teamed up with rapper Sean "Puffy" Combs on Bad Boy Records, and they dropped some of the biggest hits still playing on radios today. Tragically, BIG was murdered on March 9, 1997 in California. His death impacted so many people that they didn't just hold a memorial for him. People held a memorial/celebration of his life along the streets of his hometown, and they were playing his song, "Hypnotize," on a radio that was amplified to high volume. I have never seen so much bravado over one man's funeral! I mean, I loved the man's accomplishments, and it's a miracle that he made it to where he is remembered, but he wasn't God.

God should be given His due and credit for blessing BIG with talent. There is probably a reason God hasn't blessed us with similar talent such as Notorious BIG and other famous people who made it out of the streets into the limelight. As humans, we tend to forget the good God who has blessed us. This poem was written to show that better days will come—but we must be patient and *pray* that God will get us out of the streets.

Richmond Hill wasn't like Compton, LA—but it was bad. There were gangs running the area, and there was always news going around that someone was beaten to a pulp or that somebody had been shot. Every day, there was news—but it wasn't fresh news. It was always news of either robbery or assault. The worst part was that half of these crimes resulted from unstable home environments. If you were a boy who had a father who was involved in crime and was constantly in and out of jail, you would probably be following in his footsteps. If you had a mother who bore you when she was young and abandoned you while you were growing up, she basically drew the pattern of your life.

As a young, black man living in New York, there were really two places people expected you to be. One place was in grocery stores, cleaning or mopping after others, and the other place was prison or juvenile hall. If you did not end up in either place, you were probably dead or laid up in a hospital somewhere. Before moving to Georgia, my classmates and I applied to high schools in Queens. I wanted to go to Thomas Edison Vocational High School. All my friends were going there, and I felt that was where I would end up. Right? Wrong. Instead of Edison, I was primed to go to my zone high school, Hillcrest High. I had always heard about police cars surrounding the school and weapon detectors at the doors. To make matters worse, when people heard I was going to Hillcrest, I heard all sorts of things, such as, "You're not going to live past your freshman year," "Marc, they beat little kids like you for a hobby," or my personal favorite, "Marc, you're going to get slashed"—referring to knives and ice picks used as weapons.

Sure, I wasn't too excited about going to Hillcrest, but for the most part, I shrugged it off. I had friends at Hillcrest. I had plenty of connections, so as long as I was with them, I didn't think anything was going to happen. But then again, I didn't know the future—so I only guessed. Thank God, I moved down to Georgia that summer before entering, because if I had gone to Hillcrest, who knows what may have happened to me. Kennesaw Mountain High School was a bad experience for me in Georgia, but I know it was not worse than Hillcrest. I know for a fact that there was a Divine hand that moved in my parents' decision to move South so I would have better days ahead.

Some of you may have different stories. Some may have actually experienced life on the rough side and lost people while living there. If you made it out and you are a better person, it's by God's grace that you are serving a purpose today. If you still live in a rough, urban area and things still look bad, just remember to keep praying for your days to get better. God will deliver you.

CHAPTER 15

Can't We All Just Get Along?

Increase the Peace

Deep in the blood-soaked streets, a mother pours out her grief
as she mourns the brief existence of her son without relief
The tears proceed to flow in streams down her cheeks
As though her eye ducts are saturated faucet leaks
For weeks she dreaded this exact scene she was cast in
Now her last days will be spent weeping and fasting
Bullet hole-cracked walkways and shattered glass tell the tale
that ends in one sordid moral—as US citizens, we tend to fail
We remain frail in our efforts to cease any altercation
escalating physical situations; driving the youth to degradation
How do we, as urban people, sleep during the night?
Knowing that in plain sight, an argument evolves into a fight
Everywhere we look, we can see casualties skyrocket
Teens with black eye sockets; others with gats in their pockets
Some young blood who has the ability to succeed due to his grade
will one day meet his end at the hands of a deadly switchblade
Why do people have so little regard for the human life?
That they rip bodies with lead or run others through with a knife
Let's do our duty to ourselves and God by increasing the peace
because the next martyr may be a son, daughter, nephew, or niece
Our bodies are considered temples, so let us treat them this way
Instead of mourning the present, look forward to the next day
For the good of others, let's be both realistic and optimistic
and prevent another one of our generation from being a statistic.

A Message of Peace

With a large crowd of chief priests and soldiers behind him, Judas Iscariot, one of the twelve disciples, approached Jesus and His followers. Judas automatically gave the signal that whoever he kissed was the person who should be taken away to the governor. At this, Judas stepped forward and said, "Greetings, Rabbi!" and kissed him. Then Jesus gave Judas and the rest of his men permission to do what they came to do. They immediately arrested Jesus. One of Jesus' men took his sword out and cut off the ear of one of the chief priest's servants. Jesus told him to put his sword away. "For all who draw the sword will die by the sword."(Matthew 26:47-49)(NIV)

Even after Jesus had been betrayed by one who he had known as a brother—one of his own disciples—he still preached the message of peace. Those three verses will always humble me, because it reminds me that if I respond to violence by adding to the violent culture of today, I will end up being killed by my own weapon. If we truly reap what we sow, then whenever we commit violent acts toward one another, we are only calling for the same type of treatment upon ourselves. I wrote this poem immediately after learning that in 2009, domestic violence in urban schools had risen by 50 percent. People are showing less regard toward one another as brothers. To some people, 50 percent may not be a significant number, but to me—and especially to God—it is a *very* big deal. To me, this means that 50 percent of the time, we would rather solve our problems by hurting others and injuring others just to make a point or get our message across to society than act peacefully. What makes it worse is that these are middle school and high school students who are being counted and surveyed in the increase of violence.

Jesus tells us that not only are we to love God with all of our hearts, souls, and minds, but we must also love our neighbors as ourselves. How do we love our neighbors as ourselves if we are hurting or killing people? It is just disappointing that today's youth are resorting to acts of violence for either revenge or public attention. We did experience violence issues throughout the early 1990s, but since the new millennium began, the percentage has dropped, which is very encouraging. This shows that the youth got counseling from guidance or social workers and joined after-school programs to keep themselves away from the streets, where they are more prone to violence. When I heard the report about the rise of violence, it was very disheartening. I was fearful. I have two little brothers—one who was in high school, and one who was ready to enter high school that fall. I couldn't help but think that they were going to grow up in one of the most violent generations that this nation has ever witnessed.

Growing up in Queens, New York was no cake walk. I saw and heard terrible things that happened around me as I was growing up. One kid who went to my middle school was beaten down with a baseball bat when I was in the eighth grade. I heard he was in critical condition, but I'm not sure if he made it or not.

I had a friend in eighth grade who was from India. His name was Syed. He was a new student at the school; so naturally, people gave him a hard time. I stood by him, though, and he turned out to be a cool guy once I got to know him. Then another dude in my class gave him a much harder time than anybody else, and I kept telling this guy to leave Syed alone. So the guy left Syed alone momentarily and started messing around with me. Then it was Syed's turn to stick up for me, and he told that boy to leave me alone. The guy got upset, and he challenged Syed to fight him after school. Syed agreed, but he wanted to take the fight to a place where there would not be any teachers to break up the fight. This roughneck agreed. After school, he and Syed walked to the back of the school. I was with Syed, acting like his boxing coach, telling him to end this quickly—just a couple punches, and that was it. We tried not to make it public, but this guy kept boasting that he was going to whup Syed's butt. Soon, about half the class that remained after school showed up for the fight.

Syed was tall for his age—about six feet. The challenger was about three or four inches shorter, but he had some muscle. I remember standing right in front of the crowd before the fight. I really thought Syed had a chance, because he was taller and probably stronger. But once they started scrapping, my jaw dropped. What I saw wasn't a fight—it was a massacre. Once Syed held up his fists, indicating that he was ready to go, the guy didn't waste any time. He jumped at Syed, and with a few whirls of fists, Syed was lying on the ground, bleeding from his mouth and nose. He was too dazed to get up, and the guy who beat him spat on the ground and then stared around, like he was saying, "Who's next?" I backed away slowly, and then I went back in the school to find a nurse.

By that time, the loud screams of amazement from the kids had drawn the attention of the remaining teachers at the school, and they went and separated the crowd and took Syed to see the nurse. I passed Syed and the teacher attending to him as they walked to the nurse, and I will never forget the look he gave me. It was a look that seemed to say, "You betrayed me." It was a look of extreme resignation, and I don't think I will ever forget it. The guy who beat him up eventually transferred to a different class, but Syed never spoke to me after that incident. Time after time, I kept replaying that fight in my mind. I wondered if there was anything that I could have done to prevent my friend from getting beaten. What was worse was that a rumor spread the very next day by people describing the fight and the people who actually witnessed it. Then people remembered seeing me there and started twisting the story, stating that I had jumped in and helped the guy who beat Syed. While that boosted me in popularity points—because Lord knows, I was not popular at my middle school—I felt worse, because all of this was at the expense of my friend.

School bullying and domestic violence not only hurt people but also break friendships and trust built with one's fellow man. That is one of the reasons I have such a hard time opening up to people. It isn't that I'm shy (although I do attribute 25 percent of it to that fact), but it's because I couldn't trust anybody. I felt that everyone was out to get everyone else. I felt that it was the survival of the fittest and only the strong can survive." This was not encouraging to a skinny, thirteen-year-old kid who wore tight pants and had large bifocals hanging from his face. After seeing what happened to Syed and what was happening around me with all the gang battles, I promised myself that if I had the power to, I was going to help put a stop to it. I didn't have to join the police force or join SWAT. But I could use my words and my influence to speak up against school violence and the reasons behind it.

I heard a news report about a teenage boy in Chicago who was beaten to death while walking home from school. He didn't do anything; his only crime was being in the middle of a rival gang fight. This boy was extremely smart; he had good grades, and he was on his way to a bright future, perhaps at a Division I college. He was simply in the wrong place at the wrong time.

Another shocking detail was that this was all caught by a camera phone. The camera phone showed a recording of the boy getting hit over and over in the head with a blunt object. Even though the footage was blurry, I couldn't watch it. I hate being a witness to any type of fight. I always visualize Syed getting beat up over and over in my mind. Prior to that, if there was a fight, I would just watch—like everyone else did—so I could say I saw it. But I hated watching one of my friends fight and get beaten while I just stood and watched. It continues to numb me today.

Another reason violence is increasing is because violence is used as a form of revenge—the means of getting even with somebody. Half of this can be attributed to the media, which teaches us "an eye for an eye; a tooth for a tooth." When somebody does us wrong, we are told to repay them back twofold. But I firmly believe that two wrongs do not make a right. Even if you do exact revenge on someone who did something wrong to you, what does it accomplish? The satisfaction only lasts for a little bit, and then something called conviction steps in. It may be spiritual conviction for those who are saved, but for others, it is just conviction begat by fear of exposure and uncertainty for the future that lies ahead.

Around the same time that the young black boy was beaten to death in Chicago, a thirteen-year-old white boy was burned alive in Florida. A group of neighborhood bullies took his father's bike, and the boy reported the incident to the police. After the police confronted the bullies and gave the bike back to the boy, the bullies came over to his house and poured gasoline on him. Then they lit him on fire. Just hearing that story sickened me. The boy was sent to a burn center, where he was treated for severe third-degree burns. He survived, but if the ambulance and immediate response team had not reacted instinctively, he would have lost his life. They took off the boy's shirt, but they had to remove it carefully so they don't risk peeling off his already-burnt skin. I saw the shirt, and it was burned to a *crisp*. The police arrested the suspects, and when they were put under questioning for the burning, one of the boys laughed—as if the whole ordeal *amused* him. I've never felt angrier than when I heard that a boy got burned and his suspects just laughed when they were questioned about it. I didn't see anything funny about it. But sadly, that is what the world is coming to.

People love to see other people suffer, and it brings God pain to see His children kill and hurt each other. The night before Jesus was crucified, He knew He was going to be betrayed by one of His disciples. But Jesus did not react with violence, no matter how much His disciples wanted to retaliate. Instead, He showed another example of love by telling us that while we have the opportunity to get back at someone, it takes a bigger and better individual to let it pass and walk away, knowing that we can pray and support other people. We should show mercy to those who wouldn't do the same for us.

CHAPTER 16

I'll Die for You, but I Won't Lie for You

Ain't Got an Excuse

I ain't got an excuse for guys who act like straight-up fools
who be walkin' around school with extra cash and jewels
Dudes who be rockin' large tees and the latest headgear
People wearing a different logo with a rock in every ear
This year I ain't got an excuse for my people sleepin' in jail
who wished they could make bail and would rather be in hell
I don't control the choices people make or the steps they take
to reject those sent to free them for their own sake.
This year I ain't got an excuse for men who leave their wives
who become victims of cheaters and bribes, destroying family lives
I ain't the one who saw your man in a compromising position,
in addition to both parties living together in complete opposition
This year, I ain't got an excuse for brothas sneaking around
thinking that they need to be lost when they need to be found
We never hang or talk with them; we don't ever say a sound
Outside everything's all good; but on the inside, they're secretly bound
Then we feel sorry when they ultimately end up six feet underground
This year I ain't got an excuse for those who simply don' believe
that He came to relieve and not deceive or cause you to grieve
But instead he wants you to receive Him in faith and trust,
because you're ready and willing; not because you must.
This year, I refuse to make an excuse for those who are lost
because they don't realize the cost of eternity without the heavenly boss.

Speak for Yourself

Everyone is responsible for his or her own actions. This is the message that I was hoping to portray in this poem. We all go through problems with pride, guilt, crime, and infidelity. But just as quickly as we experience these problems, sometimes we are quicker to point fingers at others or defend those people who know they are headed down the wrong path. I wrote this poem with a burning question in mind. If somebody I knew and loved got into trouble and I knew that they were guilty of all counts, would I continue to defend them, even if my warnings beforehand were unheeded? Another question I had was whether I was responsible for the same person who got themselves in so deep that they couldn't dig themselves out. With both of these questions in mind, I wrote the piece, and I answered my own question. If I have done everything in my power to save a person from a certain situation but that person still insists on following his or her own way, I would not make any excuses for him or her in front of man or God. It's as simple as that.

I can't make excuses for people who don't make the best decisions and then end up suffering for it. If I'm your friend, and you want to do something that you know you have no business doing, I would try to convince and persuade you not to do it, with supported reasons. However, if you're just as stubborn as a mule and you won't listen to reason, I'll just see my way out and wish you good luck and Godspeed. In the first couple lines, I'll admit I got on the younger generation a little bit. I did mention clothes and jewelry, because it seems that nowadays, people are spending their hard-earned money for something that I believe serves no purpose or meaning in style, unless it means something. To tell you the truth, the way you dress is how people make their first impression of you. If you're a guy and you are wearing t-shirts and jeans three sizes too big for you in public, people's impression of you will most likely be "he's a thug" or "she's a gangsta." If you feel comfortable wearing those type of clothes, then hey, more power to you. But until you prove your worth, people will only believe what they see from the outside, because that is the way you choose to prevent yourself. Earrings, chains, watches, and different types of jewelry usually mean something.

The same goes for tattoos. I think about NBA player Allan Iverson and the controversy surrounding him because of his clothes and his tattoos. People everywhere called Allan Iverson a thug, and they judged him because he made a rap album. The NBA commissioner, David Stern, asked Allan to remove the explicit lyrics from his album. Allan Iverson chose to look and portray himself in that way, and people didn't understand him. People feared him because he was different. This happened back in the late 1990s, entering the new millennium. No one made an excuse for why Allan Iverson chose to look or sound the way he did. He made that decision himself, and he stands by his decision. But Allan Iverson proved that there was more than just a thug in him when he led the 76ers to the finals against the Lakers in 2001. People then realized that Allan Iverson, regardless of how he looked, had a heart for the game, and he took it very seriously.

If we choose to dress or look a certain way, we better be prepared to show people that there is more than what meets the eye. We better be ready to stand up for ourselves and not let anyone make excuses for our actions. Some people may think, "Oh, he dresses that way because he's a young black man and that's how they all dress; that's the way of our youth these days." That's not an excuse at all. We don't have to mimic all the hype and the media. We don't have to meet or exceed expectations—except the expectations God has set for us. For me, I dress *comfortably*. I put on a shirt that fits, jeans that fit, and if I find a pair of shoes or sneakers that I like and that are my size, that's fine with me. Clothes are not a big deal to me at all. I encourage you all not to alter your look to impress others.

Another thing we happen to make excuses for in life is infidelity. This subject gets me a bit tense at times, because when men cheat on their wives and are caught sleeping around, they tend to try to make excuses for themselves. You committed adultery because you *wanted* to; you chose to do it. No one forced you. No one coerced you into it; it was your choice. God says in His word, that he would never tempt us beyond our boundaries. This means that He will never tempt us to great to a point that we can't get ourselves out of that situation. In the story of Joseph in the book of Genesis, Potiphar's wife was tempting him, and I'll bet she used every feminine wile in the book. But Joseph knew that he was sinning against God and that adultery was wrong. If he had given in, what would he say? "She was coming on to me"? Who would believe him? He was a servant, and she was the woman of the house. Joseph probably would have been sentenced to death, but because he was honest and he stood up for himself in the name of God, Potiphar did not kill Joseph (although he sent Joseph to jail for a season). Let's not make excuses for the wrongful actions of others, but let us justify ourselves and deem ourselves honest and true to God.

CHAPTER 17

Anything Is Possible

We Too Can Fly

Here we were, tied and bound in a cramped, poorly kept ship
There was no hope for freedom as fear is the trait we grip.
Without a single clue where we were or our destination
We never would have thought that we would leave our nation
Disoriented and deranged, we arrive in a strange, new land
Where we were treated as lowlifes—below the standard of man
For four hundred years—maybe longer—were
we taken for inanimate objects
It was considered a crime to mention black and white in one subject.
In the fields, they made us work from sunrise to sunset.
Food was extremely scarce, what we had was what we get.
We felt as empty as the sacks that we carried on our backs
Trudging back to our shacks, we begin to see what we lack

We long to achieve and receive the respect of great value
It's a future that we desire, but we cannot seem to accrue
You may have fought a war over us and allowed us to vote
but we still feel even today that we are lynched by our throat
We feel the pressure of the firemen's hose as it slams us against a wall
Our skin still bears ancient whip marks; it's a wonder we survived it all
Look what we've done for you; look upon our contribution
We deserve to be viewed as mankind's infusion, not intrusion.
Over these hard years, we've learned that we succeed when we try
We've taken the fact that on God's wings, we too can fly,
Not just to the limit of the sky, but beyond high.

Keep the Dream Alive

Black people, have come a long way from where they originated and how we helped shape the nation. In the Pledge of Allegiance, there is one line in particular that stands out among the rest: "one nation under God." We say it when we are at school and at public governmental affairs—but were we always a nation under God? Throughout most of our country's history, we have fought different wars and battles. The longest battle that we have fought (and in some ways, are fighting today) is the battle for equality in America.

Despite many of the laws—including the right of black people to vote and the Civil Rights Act of 1964—our minority population still feels like the nation isn't providing black people an equal chance or opportunity to succeed in life. Up until 2010, there was never a black president in office. Before Jackie Robinson, no blacks were allowed to play in major league baseball. We not only set standards, but we broke barriers and did what other people perceived as impossible. This may be our greatest testimony, considering the fact that we did not arrive in America in style. We arrived in chains, ragged clothing on our backs, being pulled and pushed like animals, and being sold for a few pieces of silver. One thing I hated hearing when I was young was the fact that black people were sold—sold as if we were property, as if our lives are determined by how much we are worth. It was sickening. We were dragged off to fields to pick cotton and work, and the women worked as house servants and cooked and cleaned endlessly for the family.

Even Haitians can relate, because we were owned and colonized by the French before we fought for our revolution. Our situation was no different than what blacks in America experienced Were there any accomplishments in life that *we* as black people will be remembered for?

We would answer that question in the years to come. Let's take a look at all the accomplishments of different black people. Do you like potato chips? Well, the potato chip was invented by George Crum in 1853. George Crum was part Native American and part African American. He was a chef at a lodge resort in Saratoga Springs, New York. At the time, french fries were popular. One day, a customer complained that the fries were too thick. Then Crum tried to make a batch that was thinner, but the customer was still unsatisfied. Crum then cut the fries even thinner, hoping to aggravate the customer because of the complaints. The customer enjoyed the thinner fries, and soon potato chips were invented.

We definitely cannot forget Harriet Tubman, a former slave and abolitionist who conducted more than three hundred slaves through the Underground Railroad in the 1800s. She actually escaped on her own, and she had the choice to stay behind, but what made her story more captivating was that she returned to the South to risk her neck to save her people. To me, she resembled a female Moses, who fled and found freedom, but by the instruction and direction of God, came back to free her people from bondage.

Of course, we can never forget Garrett Morgan, the inventor of the traffic signal. He also invented and patented the gas mask and smoke protector for firefighters. That's crucial. Without Garrett Morgan's invention, firefighters would not be able to do their jobs to protect other people from burns and secondhand smoke, because they would be suffering from it themselves.

The world of music was also revolutionized by black people. Chuck Berry was an innovator in the music business, helping to popularize rock and roll, as well as Little Richard. The rock and roll and pop scenes were filled with white performers—all talented in their own right—but more of the white teen audiences back in the 1950s were intrigued by the talented black performers. Jackie Wilson, the Platters, and Frankie Lymon were the singers who highlighted most of the '50s. The 1960s were highlighted by R&B groups such as Smokey Robinson and the Miracles, the Supremes, and the Temptations. These groups were part of a recording label called Motown, which was also founded by a black man, Berry Gordy Jr. Jackie Wilson and Frankie Lymon also served as inspirations for a young boy who would later be known as the King of Pop. Michael Jackson and his brothers formed the Jackson 5, which was one of the biggest groups in the 1970s. Even now, there are artists sampling Michael Jackson's dance moves, such as Usher and Chris Brown.

I could go on and on about the impact of black people in music, but that would steal the point that I am trying to convey in this chapter. Black people were underestimated and underrated early in the birth of this nation, and now look at all the impact we have on this nation.

Part of the reason I started writing poetry was because I have heroes who were poets. One of my heroes is Langston Hughes. Langston Hughes was born on February 1, 1902 in Joplin, Missouri. His parents divorced when he was little, and he was raised by his grandmother. When he was thirteen, he moved to Lincoln, Illinois. He came up from humble beginnings, working at odd jobs. He published his first poetry book, *The Weary Blues*, in 1924. He went on to write many other memorable pieces influencing the jazz age and defining the Roaring Twenties. The reason I look up to Langston Hughes is that his writing helped influence and inspire a generation. His first book was released when he was twenty-two years old. I'm currently twenty-two, and I feel that I can accomplish the same goal that Langston Hughes did at my age about seventy-six years ago. I am aware things are different now, with the media and technology, but I still believe my poems and writing can make an impact for this generation and future generations.

What made Langston Hughes's legacy more intriguing were the time and people he was writing for. Slavery was gone, but there was still segregation, and there was still inequality in many places down South. In the 1960s, people were abused with fire hoses, guard dogs, and clubs. It was the most tumultuous time of that generation. Langston Hughes and Maya Angelou were the writers who opened doors for me, and I appreciate them for all they have done. Whenever I think of why our race was enslaved when we have contributed so much to society, I think of what a friend and fellow brother in Christ said. He told me, "It's man's pride and fear which leads them to do such things". Pharaoh's pride and fear of losing power were the factors of why he enslaved the people of Israel. White men feared black people. They feared our potential and power, so they enslaved us out of their own fear. They did not want to lose the power they had as lawmakers and decision-makers. I'm glad God has somewhat reduced their fears so we can live together in harmony. I cannot wait until all Christians—black or white—are together in heaven and we are united under one color—red, which signifies the blood of Christ. Together we can show the rest of the world that everyone who chooses to do so can fly.

CHAPTER 18

Thirsting for Water

All Dried Up

With our mouths parched, we arched our heads to get a sip,
our insides ripped when we realized there wasn't even a drip.
We think back to when you flowed so freely and refreshing,
the fact that you're gone leaves a feeling so depressing.
Every time we play a sport and we return wet and smell like a mess,
despite what we've been through, you made sure we looked our best
If there's a color that we could describe you as, opaque comes to mind
and you were never out of range or sight, but you were always on time
Kids can play with you, and adults look to you as a valuable asset,
you are the natural vitamin inside each fruit and vegetable basket
When you fall from the sky, you douse and arouse the tallest trees,
while you tend to wildlife's needs from the biggest bear to tiny bees
70 percent of our bodies owe you their existence and survival
in the revival of life, are you abundantly mentioned in the Bible
You are vital to us, and we would not live without your contribution
But our human nature causes confusion dealt with your retribution
When God removes you from a land, all inhabitants enter a drought
So we can learn how much we thirst for you—both inside and out.
At this time, our motherland of Haiti is suffering severe trials
I can only pray that my people can receive you in large vials
Cold, crisp, and clean, right down to the very last drop,
As with Moses, let your goodness flow out of Haiti's rock
because right now, we feel like we are all dried up,
with our throats rough and coarse; please fill our cup.

Please, Let Me Have Water

The inspiration for this poem is a rather funny one, but it is also very eye-opening. Since the devastating earthquake in Haiti, I had been experiencing writer's block for about the hundredth time. For almost two months, I couldn't write anything. It was as if the earthquake had sapped my energy and poetic mind flow. I was frustrated, angry, and honestly, a little jealous, because people I knew were writing poems and songs to remember those lost in the tragedy. Others were writing about the aid and assistance we had from other countries. I didn't understand it. I was able to write about almost every major event that has happened in the millennium. But this time I had nothing.

I didn't know what to write. I didn't have anything in me to write about this tragedy. What had been an overflowing well of words and inner thoughts was now dried up. One day, I sat at the house, wondering what I could do to retrieve the words I needed to write another poem. All through school, I kept thinking, "What am I going to write?" It wasn't until I got home and went to the bathroom to wash my hands that I once again found my inspiration. I turned on the faucet, and *nothing* came out. What was going on? I turned the faucet again. I got the same result. I went to my mother and asked her what was going on. Evidently, the water bill was not paid in time, so our water was shut off. We spent four or five hours without water. During that time, I would get so thirsty—but all we had were sugar and powder drinks, and you *need* water to make those! Thank God I had the funds to call the city water and pay the past due balance to have the water turned back on.

Even though the water was off for a short period of time, God really showed me that we cannot take His gifts and blessings for granted. Water is a gift from God—the natural element of life. Jesus even refers Himself as the Water of Life in John 4. Just a few hours with no water made me see reality. One minute without Christ is another minute that we are depriving ourselves of water—not physical water, but spiritual water. We may be well fed and healthy on the outside, but on the inside, we are dried up and withered because we allow the world to drain us of all our faith and confidence in God.

We are helping everyone in Haiti right now by feeding and nourishing them. But let us also nourish ourselves and live. I actually thank God that the water was temporarily shut off, because he has used this experience to allow my well of poetry to water up again. Now I'm back and writing stronger than ever.

CHAPTER 19

One Thing Always Leads to Another

All Because of a Little Mistake

My knees scrape as I fall and hit the asphalt,
my sudden halt reminded me that it was my fault,
I lost my job and was put on layaway.
But I saw my chance and couldn't stay away
By night, I leaped over the neighbor's wooden gate
without a clue that I was her prime bait.
I grabbed her arm as she rang the alarm
My intention was not to induce any harm
As the authorities came to try to detain me
I make one final run for my liberty
When I was cuffed, my morale began to break
All because of a little mistake.
I told my girl I loved her before we went to the car
She would say, to my deepest dismay, not to go too far
I loved everything about her, from her clothes to her fashion
She thought I was fly, and it resulted in instant passion
Ain't it funny how choices and situations ran?
How a simple "I love you" turns into a one-night stand?
I held her hand as she drifted off to sleep
I celebrated outside, but inside I weep.
Then the stunner hit—one after another
I find out my girl is gonna be a mother.
I feel like my world is crashing down
This baby was gonna turn my life around.
It was a commitment I wasn't ready for.
I'm still struggling; I'm still dirt-poor
I thought I was real, but I turned out to be fake
All because of a little mistake.

So why do I run? What do I wish to gain?
Am I really escaping from my hurt and pain?
Who can see my situation through and through?
I don't need to run away from anyone,
I need Someone to run to.

It Wasn't Intentional

Have you ever done something in your life that you knew was wrong? Did you do it anyway, not thinking about the consequences that lay ahead? Maybe it seemed like a good idea at the time—but did you end up regretting what you did when you suffered for it?

I used to hear the same thing over and over in the past. You reap what you sow. For every action, there is an equal and opposite reaction. That was one of Newton's laws of gravity and motion. It can also apply to everyday life. No matter what we do in life, our action is always linked back to us. Even if it wasn't on purpose—even if it was a so-called accident or mistake—we end up paying for it in the long run. Our mistake in life is that for everything that *we* do, we blame God for the repercussions rather than accepting the blame ourselves.

In this poem, I mentioned two different scenarios in which people are either forced or tempted to make the biggest mistake of their lives—and they end up losing much more than their self-respect. Lives are altered, and we take a part in denying or running away from our problems. In the beginning, the character is running away from his problems. He's running away from his responsibility. He's running right into the arms of fear. Some people, due to financial reasons, are forced to become small-time crooks and steal from homes. Thanks to modern-day home security, this has become less of an issue. But that does not mean it's not being attempted today. There may be some people in life who are forced against their will to rob homes. Others just enjoy taking things from those more privileged. Whatever the reason may be, theft just paves a path to the ruin of lives and erases any chance for the thief to have a fulfilling life. The worst thing is that when young people get arrested and go to prison, there is slim to no chance that those individuals will have a good career. Even among young black men, there is a zero chance of redemption once they've been in jail (unless you're famous or are some type of athlete).

At the First Baptist Church of Jonesboro, we had a youth preacher come every fourth Sunday and preach to our youth group. On one particular Sunday, he gave a testimony about one of his best friends who he grew up with. He started out going to church every Sunday, and then when he was in middle school, he started stealing from grocery stores. As he got older, he started to commit grand theft auto, stealing cars for dealers and hustlers. He even tried to convince the preacher to join him in his jobs, but even though the youth preacher was not saved at the time, he did not want to join his friend to live a life of crime. Shortly afterwards, the preacher's friend was arrested for felony charges and served a 5 year sentence in prison. Eventually he was released, but his life was basically in pieces. He would have to struggle to make ends meet—and most jobs would not hire ex-cons.

The training of a little boy starts at home. If the parents are not aware of who their children are associating with or do not care to ask or talk to their kids, they end up suffering much worse than the child in the long run. I'm aware that as teens, most people want their parents or guardians to be as distant as possible. But fulfilling that wish is only hurting your child, not helping him. If

I got caught in a sticky situation in life, my parents were always there to clear it up. We must not be too proud or ashamed to run to the experienced when we find out we are in grave danger.

Another scenario is perhaps the most sensitive subject in this book: premarital sex. Personally, I believe in abstinence and waiting for marriage, because the Bible instructs it. I see so many problems that arise out of sex before marriage. First of all, there is fear—fear of exposure, fear of early pregnancy, fear of sexually transmitted diseases, and the most dreaded of all, fear of commitment. Speaking from a male point of view, I am not going to lie—in fact, I'm going to put it as plainly as possible. Men love sex. Men love the feeling—the groping, the intensity of two bodies expressing one similar thing, the lustful passion. How many times do men think about sex? Popular articles and some sites say that men think about it every eight seconds. Whether that's true or not, one thing is certain—men most likely are more aggressive in initiating sexual contact. If men are dating other women or engaging in physical contact, they make the first move about 65 percent of the time.

Another negative consequence of premarital sex is that it is completely physical. There is no love, no commitment, and no bond. Sure, there is a physical bond, but no spiritual bond. If one mate does not know the other, then they will move on and make one-night stands a habit. Before you make a decision to get sexually or intimately involved, make sure both you and your partner are spiritually and emotionally involved. Let us think about our actions and think about the people we are hurting—and the King we are hurting. In the long run, little mistakes will catch up to us all. Without the mercy of Christ, it will be impossible to continue running to Him and for Him.

CHAPTER 20

Taking that Leap of Faith

Airborne

My stomach's in knots as I wait at the gate
checking my watch to make sure I ain't late
I haven't flown yet since I was the age of three
I wonder what was even in store for me
Across me I notice a beautiful girl waiting as well
My mouth nearly fell, because she wasn't a typical Southern belle,
Before I can get too cozy, a voice in the speaker blared
stating that in forty minutes we'll be up in the air
People lined up in queue to board the confident jet
but you can bet that it wasn't time to leave yet
I move toward my seat as quickly as I could go
Then I realized they've given me a seat next to a window!
Petrified was I, but I had no time to whine or mourn
as the plane went fifty, sixty, seventy, eighty,
ninety—then we were airborne
I stared out the window as the building got smaller
I sat and relaxed, feeling taller as my faith grew stronger
When I leaned back to fully enjoy my flight,
I knew that everything was going to be all right.

It's All about Letting Go

It's funny how God can use regular scenarios such as flying an airplane to speak to others. This poem was written following the flight from Atlanta, Georgia to JFK Airport in Queens, New York. I was sitting at the Hartsfield-Jackson Airport, waiting at my gate until I boarded the flight. I don't think I'd ever been that nervous before—after all, this was going to be my first time flying an airplane since I was three years old and I flew to Haiti with my mother to visit my grandmother. It didn't make it any better that I was asleep whole flight and that I only remember about 33 percent of the trip.

I felt straight-up sick to my stomach. I guess all the news reports regarding plane accidents were finally getting to me. Two weeks before I left, I heard the news report of a plane crash around Buffalo, New York. I would try to psych myself out telling myself, "Why are you tripping over one plane ride? You know God's got you, and He won't allow anything to happen." One week before I left, my brothers and I decided to have a movie night, as we occasionally do. My brothers were fans of suspense, horror, and thrill, so what movie did they *have* to choose? They had to get *Final Destination*. In the beginning of the movie, a high school kid had what people thought was a hallucination of the plane crashing upon takeoff. But rather than being a hallucination, it was actually a premonition that the plane was going to crash, and he shrieked, broke into a cold sweat, and had to be let off the plane. Six others followed him off the plane. As soon as the plane took off without the seven passengers, the kid's premonition came true, and the plane exploded in midair, killing everybody on board. I couldn't believe I watched that movie before I had to go. A month before that, I watched *We Are Marshall,* in which Marshall University's entire football team was killed in a plane crash and a new, strange, innovative coach had to rebuild the team.

All those images of plane crashes came to my head, and I had the urge to get up and just cancel my trip. *That's the devil,* I thought. *He doesn't want me to go. He's using the media and world influence to stall my faith and attack me so I won't go through with it.* That's what Satan does and strives to do to everyone—especially the followers of Christ. He replays the worst-case scenario in your head so you no longer trust Christ. Once he knows your faith is gone, he moves subtly into your heart, mixing fear and doubt into a potion of misconception. We see that Satan frequently attacks the followers of Christ simply for that reason—we are following Christ. Satan knows that to be on the same plateau with Jesus, you have to believe in Jesus through faith.

For example, take the passage found in Matthew 14 where Jesus ordered His disciples to take a boat and sail to the other side while he separated the crowd. This was right after He fed five thousand hungry souls. The boat the disciples were in sailed further and further away from shore. In the middle of the night, Jesus walked on water as He went to meet them. His disciples were terrified, screaming, "It's a ghost!"(Matt. 14:26) (NIV) Jesus immediately said to them, "Take courage! It is I. Don't be afraid." Peter, one of the disciples, was not convinced and asked Jesus to prove it was Him by having Jesus ask him to come to Him on the water. Jesus said one word, "Come." Peter came out of the boat and began walking on water toward Jesus. His eyes were fixed to go to his Savior. But then Peter's faith wavered. He saw the winds, was afraid, and began to sink.

Satan started to appeal to Peter's physical senses, because spiritually, Peter was so drawn to Jesus that he did not know that what he was doing at the time was humanly possible. The body of water Peter walked on wasn't a small lake or pool someone could stand up in. This was an ocean—a very deep ocean, at that. No mortal man could walk it. But Jesus was not just a mortal man. He was much more than that. He was the Son of the living God. Nothing is impossible to Jesus, and as long as we keep our eyes fixed on Him, nothing is impossible for us, either. But if we our faith starts to waver, like Peter's did, then we are going to start sinking into this world's troubles and the heartache and pain this world brings.

When Jesus saw Peter sinking, Jesus reached out and caught him. This is what I love about our Lord and Savior. If we ever start sinking into our own sinful quicksand, He is there to reach out with His loving hand to help us get back on our feet. Jesus then asked Peter, "You of little faith, why did you doubt?" Why did I doubt an amazing opportunity God put before me to return home and minister in Queens? Why didn't I reach out to grab my Savior's hand? Why didn't I put the flight in His hands? God finally made me see sense that day, and I boarded the plane, brimming with confidence, knowing and believing that God was with me. Nothing the Devil could dish out at me could shake my confidence and faith.

PART 4

Relationships, Intimacy, and Marriage

"Love is patient, love is kind. It does not envy, it does not boast, it is not proud. It is not rude, it is not self-seeking, it is not easily angered; it keeps no record of wrongs"

(1 Corinthians 13:4–5)(NIV).

CHAPTER 21

Be Intimate, not Intimidated

What Is Intimacy?

Intimacy requires more than just physical body contact
displaying affection to people of all genders, white or black
It's a fact that intimacy is more than a chance meeting
upon greeting, it's the look that you share, so fleeting
not deceiving, but receiving as love and sensitivity is interceding
Intimacy is allowing her to see past your outer desire and pride,
about opening yourself up and allowing him to enter inside
your mind, so divine, as your body longs for the ethereal,
a feeling so imperial it surpasses any physical material
Your spirits are on the same page as your bodies connect
Just as two opposite roads that intersect into one more perfect
Intimacy is stating your absolute love without speaking
when both of your words flow out as natural as breathing
Intimacy is passion bred for satisfaction and pleasure
To find as treasure once lost but regained at the greatest measure
Intimacy is not merely feeling loved or performing the act
it is an antidote for the soul when hate and anger attack
When denial meets trials in a cruel world so vile,
Intimacy makes living this life much more worthwhile.

Being Intimate

Intimacy is a feeling of closeness and connection generated between people as a result of a strong mutual intention to share feeling, understanding, and communication. This may or may not include sexual interaction or closeness. Being intimate with someone else requires time to share and understand the person you are intimate with. When you are intimate with someone, they look past all your shame, guilt, and shortcomings. The past is no longer relevant, because the relationship focuses so much on the here and now.

When I drove to work one day, I played the usual gospel station on the way. There was one lady on the radio who broke down the meaning of the word *intimacy* and helped me make more sense out of the word. When you split the words into four syllables, it comes out to be *int–i–ma–cy*—allowing someone to *see into my soul*. This means that the person you are intimate with has to know what your needs are. He or she has to be there to comfort you when you feel angry or sad. Even when the person you are intimate with doesn't tell you the reason he or she feels that way, something within him or her draws you close. Intimacy is about having a sixth sense for what your loved ones want and desire. It's about having the heart, courage, and most importantly, the love to make sure they are always laughing and comforted when you are with them.

Intimacy is also defined as "the absence of fences as both partners—man and woman—experience familiarity and closeness."(Webster's Ninth New Collegiate Dictionary) There are no fences. With your loved one, there are no secrets. Once your loved one spills their secrets to you—what makes him or her laugh, cry, what angers or hurts him or her—that person has shared a little bit of his or her soul with you. The trust that person has for you begins to break down the fence of distrust and doubt.

Some people have experienced abusive relationships in their lives, and they have built fences so high that no matter who they encounter in the future, they never regain that same sense of intimacy. This is why time is so essential in an intimate relationship. The person with the abusive past needs time to heal and time for God to work in her heart and reveal to her that not all guys are physically intimidating and violent. For a man to force the issue is not going to help at all. Men cannot force a woman to trust them immediately—especially after the woman gets out of an abusive relationship.

Have you ever heard the saying, "the bigger they are, the harder they fall"? Year after year, some women go through life, putting on a mask and acting as if everything is okay, when in fact, they are suffering. Men need to imitate the Man who has shown the greatest example of love to us—Jesus Christ. In Luke 8:41-56, Jesus was received by crowds that were waiting for Him. A man approached Jesus with the sad news that his twelve-year-old daughter was dying. The man prayed that Jesus would heal her.

As Jesus followed the man to his house, there was a woman who had a hemorrhage in her system for twelve years. She had spent everything she had on the doctors, but she still could not find a cure. She heard that Jesus was going to be in town, and she knew that Jesus had the power to heal. She came up behind Jesus and simply touched His robe. Her bleeding stopped immediately. Jesus felt it, because he asked, "Who touched me?" Peter, his disciple, reminded Him that He was among a crowd of people and that everyone was touching him. Yet Jesus *felt* the touch of the sick, bleeding woman. The woman, realizing that Jesus knew what she did, was scared and fell to her knees. She explained why she touched Jesus. Jesus replied, "Daughter, your faith has made you well. Go in peace."

Jesus knew that the greatest gift you can give a person is love. Of course, because He was God incarnate, he was able to heal the bleeding woman, but it was the *mercy, grace,* and *understanding* that set Jesus apart from other men. If the woman had touched the robe of one of the religious leaders of that day, they would have thrown her off to the side like she was of no significance.

Women *need* to be touched—not only physically, but spiritually and emotionally. Women nowadays resemble the bleeding woman in the Bible, because they have been suffering so intensely in the past that they need someone to *touch* them; they need someone to share their suffering. Women need to share their souls with the right person. If a relationship is only based on the physical aspects, there is no real connection, and the relationship will not survive. Just because you are intimate sexually does not mean that you are in an intimate relationship.

If a woman cannot rely on a man for trust, love, support, and guidance, the relationship will die. If a man cannot show the maturity, dignity, or sensitivity to be someone to confide in or hold on to, the relationship will die. If a man and woman cannot be *one* with each other and feel what the other person is feeling, intimacy is not in the relationship. Intimacy needs to be taken seriously. Intimacy needs to be taken into consideration for your man or your woman. God needs to be established in the relationship, because if both men and women can hold on to Jesus, He will bring people closer to each other in intimacy and love.

CHAPTER 22

How I Wish that it Would Rain

As the Rain Pours

Nature's shower continues to fall as I stare at the sky in vain
wishing that the rain could wash away all my present pain
Pain of being rejected once again by my social group
who took me on an emotional ride that ended in a loop
as I sit aloof, thinking about the rain falling outside
Hopelessness abides as I miss those who were once by my side
Some say rain represents God's tears as He sheds His somber mood
But to the plants and other life forms, rain is nature's food
To me, rain is just a reflection of my self-esteem,
I seem to fall wherever I land, then flow upstream.
Following the hills and slopes of this rugged earth,
Sometimes I feel like I follow others without any worth
Other times, as the rain pours, I think about her
Thoughts of her keep me warm and cozy like nature's fur
Through the monsoon, all I think about is her smile
Just the gift of communing with her makes it worthwhile
And even though the rain pours, there is no dark cloud
Her words comfort me and cover me like a shroud
As the rain pours, I think back to my younger years
When I would run through the rain without any fears
Hoping to catch a raindrop and feel the moisture on my face
Basking in the glory and blessing of God's divine grace
Everything is green and serene when the rain pours.

Can Rain Really Wash Away Pain?

My mind really ran with me on this one. On a regular day, when it rained outside, it would have little to no significance to me whatsoever. Up to the point at which I wrote this piece, rain only did two things to me—it made me either gloomy or sleepy. But there was something special about the time that I wrote this poem, because I was in Atlanta, Georgia, and we were experiencing a long stretch during which we had rain nonstop for about two weeks. I wouldn't call it a monsoon, exactly, but it wasn't far off. It was the first time I witnessed this happen. I've seen it rain for two or three days at a time, but never before has it rained for *weeks* at a time. The most baffling thing was that the rain never seemed to let up. It kept on *pouring* and *pouring* and *pouring.* It's a good thing my house was in the middle of a hill and we had gutters along the sides of the road and little places where the water would run off. Places that were on flat ground, however, were not that fortunate. Many bridge passageways and public areas were flooded. Even Ryla experienced flooding in the parking lot, and the company had to call the employees out to move their cars from the flooded areas and park on higher ground. There was just something *different* about this type of rain shower.

When it kept on raining this way, God had me thinking—not about one thing, but about a series of events. My mind never had so much in it as it did at that time. I was thinking about all the negativity that surrounded me—yet I was also thinking about all the positive things in life. The reason I placed this poem in this section is because when I finished writing the poem, I understood that rain is a sign of God's love for us. Rain is a gift from God that is sent to water and nourish His green earth. God didn't have to send rain down to us; what did we do to deserve it? We only use His name in vain, worship other things, and give material valuables more importance than Him. We break God's law every day—yet He still sends rain. I will never know why—except that it is through His grace.

There was a period when the people of Israel did evil before the eyes of God, and God did not send rain for an extended amount of time. If you look throughout the Old Testament in 1 Kings or 2 Kings, the land was in drought until Elijah prayed to God for rain and rain fell on the land. This was immediately after the challenge with the prophets of Baal. God had me thinking about my life in general through the rain, because though it was raining, part of me still felt like I was in a drought. I thought back to the times when I was used by my so-called "friends," and then after I was of no use to them, I was discarded. I had one friend call me his cousin at one point, because we were close—probably closer than I was with my own brothers. We went on trips together, witnessed the good news together, and even hung out at each other's house. Then he got a girlfriend, and things changed. I didn't have any problems with his girlfriend, and she never tried to get between us. But I was hurt and offended when I wasn't invited to his wedding—not even as a guest. This was the guy who called me his cousin—his brother. I always invited him over to my house; I was always there when he needed me. Whenever he needed me to read some type of poem, I was there for him. I treated him like he was my *brother*, and he went off, madly in love with his girlfriend. I was left out to dry.

I tried to hide my feelings, but I couldn't help it. Being rejected hurts, and I was only human. Sticks and stones did hurt, and he threw a boulder right at my head. I wasn't angry at him only, but what he did brought up unhappy memories from the past where I was always being used by people because I couldn't do anything about it. If my friends weren't there, I was just a short, skinny boy who couldn't hack it.

I thought about it, but for some reason—whether it was God or not, I wasn't sure—I thought about someone I was very fond of back in New York. This girl and I knew each other for a long time, and I'll admit that I had a crush on her. She knew it—but I think she used that to have an emotional edge on me. We went to the same church, Bethany, and she would give me a hard time, just teasing me and making fun of me. I would just sort of grin and bear it, because I couldn't bring myself to insult her; that's how much love I had for her. Before I moved, she was one of the last people I saw in New York. I knew that inside the seemingly tough exterior, she had a heart that Jesus loved. She had a heart that *I* loved—and still love today.

In my first year of using Facebook, she was one of the first people I tried searching for. I finally succeeded in getting her as a friend. When I saw her again, I was taken aback. She had become more beautiful than I remembered. I was (and in some ways, still am) contending with my feelings. Is it love or lust? It can't be lust, because I'm not merely attracted to her body. There is much more I wanted to know about her, and hopefully, God will give me a chance someday. But I thank God for our friendship, and I wouldn't give it up for anything, because good friends are hard to find. If God should somehow bring us together, let His will be done. But if not, that will be okay as well. I will still love and trust God in the end.

Finally, I thought about when I was a kid. I would go out into the rain and try to catch as many drops on my tongue as possible. I know it sounds dumb, but just like other curious kids out there, I wanted to taste the rain. I wanted to feel the rain run down my face. I wanted to know what it was like to get that water from heaven.

Any time you hear the soft *pitter-patter* of raindrops on your roof or on the ground, just think about how much God loves you. Think about how much more you can benefit from Him. Allow the rain to wash away all doubt and all your fear and anger. Allow the rain to wash away any sickness or remorse for the past and for your desires. We can learn from our past and present when the rain pours.

CHAPTER 23

What's Love Got to Do with It?

Waiting on You Is Hard

I was prepared and set to be your one true friend and lover
They say you can't always judge a book by its cover.
On the outside you appear to be as sweet as honey
but your devious heart is after my talent and money.
You continue to induce me and seduce me
but out in public, you won't even introduce me
Your lips long and wait to be kissed with bliss
as you persist to demonstrate what I'll miss
When I stare deep into the windows of your soul
I feel like I'm looking into a deep, dark, black hole
Your goal is to have me wrapped in your rope of lies
But one day, out of the ashes of our love, my worth will rise
I can't just settle and wait for you to meet me halfway
So don't let my night ruin your seemingly perfect day
Perhaps it'd be better if you walked your own way without delay
When you're solitary and alone, you'll learn to appreciate me
whether it takes a millisecond or an entire eternity
No matter what happens between us, you're still in my heart
even after I've been shot by your lethal love dart
I still have love for you, but waiting on you is hard
One day, you'll love me the best way that you can
for who I am—a true, honest, real man.

"For the lips of an adulteress drip honey
and smoother than oil is her speech
But in the end she is bitter as wormwood,
sharp as a two-edged sword" (Proverbs 5:3–4).

Is She for Real?

Throughout this book, I've always done my best to respect women and to be thankful that God has created lifelong companions so that men would not have to endure this tough life alone. I've been nice to the women thus far, and I would love to keep it that way. But in this chapter, I'm going to have to get real with the ladies. Don't consider this stereotypical or chauvinistic, but consider this tough love and hard truth. Not all women are honest.

Yeah, I said it, and I'll repeat it again. Not all women are honest. Some women act like they are helpless and sweet, and then when a man gets to know a woman better, his trust for the woman begins to increase. Sadly, so do the secrets and the silent overspending on her behalf. Instead of becoming one soul, as the Lord has ordained it, the man's soul is trapped within the woman's web of intrigue and deception. Not all women are like that, but some women are. I keep hearing the saying, "Don't worry, Marc, there are a lot of other fish in the sea," but silently I'm thinking, *Yeah, right.* The women aren't the fish, in my opinion. Men are the fish at times, because they allow any scantily clad woman in to seduce them with her words. Before a man knows it, he's hooked by her feminine wiles, and she reels him in. Then it's dinnertime! A woman like this eats up a man's money, self-respect, dignity, and before he knows it, she will have eaten up a chunk of his life as well. Then, when she has picked him dry, she moves on to the next fish.

Proverbs plainly describes the adulteress in clear, unadulterated fact. Proverbs 5:3 tells us that the lips of an adulteress drip honey, and her speech is smoother than oil. When a man kisses a woman, he loves the feel of her lips. The scent of her hair is intoxicating. Both people are in their little worlds, and the man is oblivious to anything around him. When a woman whispers dirty secrets in a man's ears, it arouses him and excites him. He gets turned on, and as the woman's body language shifts to the left, so does the man's. Men get so caught up in the physical presence of women that it's like a drug to them, blocking and impairing their better judgment. For all the music fans out there, who can forget the song written by members of the New Edition group, Bel Biv Devoe (BBD), called "Poison"? While the song is secular, it is true in some ways. Some women are like poison—and just like poison, they can be lethal.

I look at athletes nowadays, and the fact that they are athletes does not prevent them from committing adultery with women who enjoy lying with them to gain bragging rights and money in return. I think about NBA star Kobe Bryant, who committed adultery with a nineteen-year-old girl in Denver, Colorado. The girl then turned around and accused Bryant of rape. Bryant said that he did not rape her, but that he did have a sexual encounter with her that was consensual. Bryant is just one victim among many.

Earlier this year, Tiger Woods was discovered having multiple affairs with women outside his marriage. That may have shocked people more than anything, because when people think of Tiger Woods, they think, *Oh, well, he's a humble golf player with a couple of endorsements for Gatorade and Hanes, and he just minds his business. There's no way Tiger Woods would ever be caught in a sticky situation like that.* It surprised many people. But I wasn't surprised, because I knew that both Kobe Bryant and Tiger Woods are *human.* They still made mistakes, and even though they paid for them in their own way, it didn't change my opinion of them as athletes.

Proverbs 5 continues by saying that at the end, an adulteress is as bitter as gall and as sharp as a two-edged sword. It also says "her feet go down to death; and her steps lead straight to the grave. She gives no thought to the way of life"(Proverbs 5:4) (NIV). This should already give the guys a clue—especially guys who claim to be Christians. If a woman gives no thought to the way of life, she is not thinking about Jesus. If Jesus claims to be the way, the truth, and the life, then that's who He is. It may seem harsh, but once again, it's tough love. An adulteress does not have any thoughts of Jesus in her heart, because all she is concerned about is dragging others down to her own personal destruction. Unless an adulterous woman repents of her ways, chooses to follow Christ, and tries to find the image of Christ in the right man, she has no other way to eternity or living a healthy life.

Another classic Bible example of an adulteress is Delilah in Judges 16. The judges mentioned in the Bible are not the judges you see on TV with the big gavel, long black robes, and nice hair (some with terrible TV reality shows). These judges were powerful men and women who were appointed by God to lead Israel into battle, teach the people the ways of God, and help the people obey His word. This was God's way of training Israel for a king. Before there were kings, the judges ruled the land.

One particular judge, Samson, was the strongest and the most popular. His strength came from the power of God through his hair. Samson had explicit directions not to cut his hair. Samson kept this promise to God, and God gave him many victories over the Philistines, who were the enemies of God's people. However, Samson's faith in God constantly wavered, because he disobeyed God on many levels. His rule over Israel may be described as inconsistent. He usually hung out with the Philistines as friends, and he married a Philistine woman, which was against Israel's customs. After his wife was killed, Samson fell in love with Delilah, and Delilah had Samson hooked. The Philistine rulers saw this as an opportunity to finally defeat Samson once and for all, and they told Delilah to try and find out what the source of Samson's strength was. Samson lied to her three times before telling her that all his strength was in his hair. So Delilah lured Samson to sleep (she probably sang some lullaby!), and while Samson was asleep, the Philistines came into the room and cut off Samson's hair. When Samson woke up, he realized his strength was gone, and the Philistines finally subdued him. Samson would eventually avenge his enemies, but because of his inconsistency and his trust in Delilah, he lost his life.

Samson was a man of God, and even he fell into the same trap that most men fall into today. Here's the real question: how can you find a virtuous, wise woman of God? Proverbs 31 explains the perfect, ideal woman of God—a woman of intelligence, noble character, and grace. To me, the verse says that a woman of noble character and upstanding faith does not *have* to dress in revealing clothes or entice men with her looks to attract attention. A woman of noble character has *faith* in herself; she knows she's beautiful and smart. I like Proverbs 31:29–20, which say, "Charm is deceptive; and beauty is fleeting; but a woman who fears the Lord is worthy to be praised." If you are a woman who loves God, loves herself, and loves others, that's good enough for me. Even if you have not received Christ as your personal Savior, if you believe in grace, mercy, patience, and caring, you are also a strong woman in your own right. A wise man would seek out a woman of that character, and God will bring both together and form a bond that can last forever. A foolish man only goes after what he can *see*, but a wise man goes after what he *knows* and *trusts*. Remember that when you look for a special someone to spend the rest of your life with. Even though waiting for the right person is hard, when the right person comes, it is always well worth the wait.

CHAPTER 24

I Need You Now

Longing for Love

Have you ever wanted something so much that it burned?
Then you suddenly learn that it's love that you yearn
You suddenly feel trapped, cornered, and concerned
Instead of a beautiful rose, you're just a plain fern
Have you wanted something so bad—something you had
that when you didn't get it, you felt sad or even mad
You sit there clothed in your shroud of anger and doubt
searching for an alternative—searching for a way out
Have you ever loved someone who was out of your reach
leaving your soul impeached; smelling like distilled bleach
You wait for her to stop at your block and give a care
but she walks on like you were never really there.
You stand there as you heart rips out of your chest;
you come to terms, because you've given love your best
Like the Jew who lay beaten at the side of the road,
You wait for that Samaritan to fix your broken love load
Ask yourself why it hurts to long for true love
The answer still lies with the Father in heaven above
I've longed for someone to call my own for years
Someone to alleviate my pain and chase away all fears
I'm still longing for you—whoever you are
Wherever you may be, I know you're not far.

I Need Your Love

She loves me; she loves me not. She loves me; she loves me not. I didn't know what I thought. It was the spring semester of 2002, and I was a freshman at Kennesaw Mountain High School. I was at health class, and there was a beautiful girl sitting right across from me. Since I moved down to Georgia, she had been the only good thing about the school. The way she walked and talked and carried herself was irresistible. I'll never forget her name—*Jeanne*. She was smart, and sophisticated—and did I mention that she was fine? She was *fine!* But little did I know that I was playing way out of my league. The reason she didn't act like the other girls in the class was because she wasn't a freshman. She was a junior, and it was unfortunate that I found out after I tried to ask her out.

Class was over, and we were headed out to the bus port to go home. I caught up with her and I tried to ask her. Suddenly, my mouth was stuck in mid-sentence. *Come on, man!* I thought to myself. I had to get myself together. When I finally stammered out the words and asked her if she wanted to hang out on the weekend, she simply laughed, looked at me like I was insane, and walked off. That was the *first* time in my life I had been rejected by any girl. It was probably my fault. I should've buckled down and manned up. But what happens in the past stays there, so there was not much I could do.

I learned something important that day. If you fall in love, do not let love consume you or turn you into its slave. All of us long for love, one way or the other—whether it's being loved by your husband, your wife, your kids, or your parents. There is someone whose love is unconditional, and we will never have to long for it. That someone is Jesus Christ, and He loves us so much that He died on the cross for our sins. No physical love that I have for anyone else on earth can replace that love that Christ has for us. Rather than chasing love, why not let people *see* the *love of Christ* in you? Allow love to come to you. Just as Jesus spreads His arms to show His sheep His guidance and protection, let us show that same love toward our wives and husbands and respect them for the people they are. Jesus has given me a reason not to long for love, because He loves me. When He thinks I'm ready, He will bring someone my way through prayer and faith. Jesus has shown us what he has said in John 13:15: "Greater love has man than this that he lay down his life for his friends" (NIV). Because of that, I will never be ashamed to tell anybody I love them and that they are brothers and sisters in the body of the Most High.

CHAPTER 25

Do I Know You?

Stranger in the House

Your heart skips a beat when you first meet the man,
There's definitely heat between you that you don't understand.
At first you draw so close to him that you'll never let go
He begins to tell you things that he would never let anyone know
Sprung and head over heels, you then decide that he's the one
But he has no idea what he got himself into or what he's done
He doesn't realize that a commitment requires preparation,
that a broken vow after a union would equal slow restoration.
In a subliminal state he took your ready hand to wed,
just so he can secure the right to take you to bed,
you don't see what lies ahead as you lie by his head,
thinking about a perfect future—but the opposite came instead.
Unaware of his background, you take him at his word every time
not noticing that every word that comes out is just another play line
He no longer shares the love that you try to express him
The joint of marriage you two created suffers a broken limb
Now your futures look dim as trust gives way to lies and hate
as you distance yourself from your mate with each passing date
But as days turn into months, and months turn into years
Your lives produce nothing more than guilt, bloodshed, and tears
One day your worst fears are confirmed as you learn the truth
You spot him lying with another woman as you enter an emotional booth
You try your best to conceal, but it's been revealed like her open blouse,
All this time, you've been living with a stranger in the house.

Who Are You?

In one way or another, we always find ourselves asking that question about our husbands, wives, girlfriends, or boyfriends. You may have been with your significant other for weeks, months, or even years, but for some reason, you see or hear something about that person that makes you question, "Who did I get involved with?"

When this poem was posted onto Facebook, it was the most popular poem that I have posted, drawing various comments and opinions about infidelity. Even if people did not comment, it probably made them think before diving headfirst into a serious relationship. This poem was one of the many pieces where my mind just ran with me. I felt that God wanted me to write it because of the rising rates of divorce in America. Divorce rates have steadily risen in the US, and it is of great concern not only to God, who ordained marriage as being an inseparable bond between man and woman, but also to many couples who have already married once and then divorced. Can a woman learn to trust another man again? Can a man learn to settle down for just one woman? About a quarter of the US population has married and divorced once, with about 10 percent divorcing twice.

One day, I thought I needed to get to the bottom of why divorce rates were rising. For one thing, divorce rates may be rising thanks to the wonderful world of media (once again)! When people see high-profile actors and actresses marry and then divorce after only a couple months, this is teaching them that the only way to deal with a bad relationship is to walk away and move on to the next one. Rarely do you see or hear TV, magazines, or the radio encourage couples to resolve their issues and marital problems. What you *do* see is talk shows that do nothing but bring those disputed lovers on national TV to bring their business out there and further degrade themselves. I'm not going to lie. I was a fan of Jerry Springer back in the 90s, with all the chants of *"Jerry, Jerry, Jerry!"* I used to see it as entertaining—but when I knew better, I saw that the show only made matters worse. It wasn't enough that instead of turning to God and the family unit, someone would turn to a complete stranger, and then that person's problems were out live on mainstream cable. When I saw the reality of it, I stopped watching the show, because it was morally and spiritually degrading. Can you imagine meeting someone who has the same interests as you, likes to do the same things you do, enjoys the same food, and makes you feel really good about yourself—only to find out years later that you never really knew the person's nature?

Another reason for divorce is that we never take the *time* to know our partners. We came, we saw, we married—that's basically what we tend to do. We are impatient. Ladies are not looking for Mr. Right. They want Mr. Right-now-and-here—a couple of dates here and there, the man pays for the woman's meals, pulls the chair behind her, puts on a real "gentleman show," and then she's sprung. Then after a few months—or at most, a year—of dating, he pops the question. Unless there is a good reason, she feels that this is right, and she can't turn him down. So she accepts, gets engaged, and gets married. Then the mask comes off. It may come off in many ways. One way the mask comes off is in force. One thing I hate more than anything in a world is seeing a man hit his wife. How can men hit or strike the being God sent to them as a companion and helper? I don't understand it, and there is no excuse for it.

Abuse is one way to end a marriage fast, quick, and in a hurry. I've seen many Lifetime movies in which women are being abused by their husbands or boyfriends. The worst thing we can do is stand there and let it happen. If we see abuse or evidence of abuse, we need to report it and help the people out as soon as we can before the matter gets worse. One thing I vowed to myself and to Jesus is that I will never hit my wife. I just can't stoop that low.

The mask may also be taken off in revelation. You may come home from work or school and see another car outside your house. You don't think much about it. You think maybe your husband or wife has some friends over. You open your front door and walk up to your bedroom, completely unprepared for what you are about to see. There is your husband or wife in bed, between the sheets with another man or woman. Rage boils inside of you. First, you feel betrayed, and then you feel uncontrollable anger. With those events in motion, a marriage union is pretty much in shreds.

How do you prevent that from happening? Get to know your partner better. Date and go to some social events for about two or three years—maybe four. That gives you time to know the pros and cons of the person you are with. Remember that if you divorce one and marry another, it's against the Bible. Matthew 19:9 says, "I tell you that anyone who divorces his wife, except for marital unfaithfulness and marries another woman commits adultery" (NIV). Remember, marriage is a two way-street, with both positives and negatives involved. Look both ways before you cross and make a commitment.

CHAPTER 26

All That I Am

All of Me

My eyes would suddenly double up when I see your face
Time and space can't erase your aura and your grace.
I remember when it was cold and you curled up under my arm
and I was your bodyguard and kept you from harm.
Every time you cried, I was there to brush away your tears
When things went bump in the night, I extinguished your fears
I never had a lot of money, but I was rich because I had you
Even though I lie about some things; to you, I was always true to,
just like you, during your struggles, I always felt your pain
But my love is like an umbrella that keeps you dry from the rain
With my love, I receive you; with my humility, I concede to you
With my heart and soul, I promise never to deceive you.
Nothing else in the world matters but your soft touch
because I still have strong feelings for you very much
When you left me, you walked away with all my emotion,
Now I'm here to grant you complete, endless devotion,
in a vast ocean filled with doubt, betrayal, and uncertainty
I don't want you to have just 50 percent; I want you to have all of me,
Our love can be free of all hate, negativity, and future guilt,
we can take our passion to a place where it'll never wilt
where it can be rebuilt with the pillars of our dedication.

Show Them the Soft Side

In the previous chapter, I explained some of the reasons most marriages end in divorce. I listed almost every reason except one important reason: the absence of love and sensitivity. Husbands do not show the love or concern to their wives in this day. I'm going to get on the guys now. Gentlemen, if we want to keep our marriages or relationships going strong, we are going to have to be sensitive and show that we care about what our women want. This doesn't mean serving women without any dignity or pride for ourselves, but it does mean that we have to care about *us* all the time.

If you are in a relationship or are married, it's not about *you*. It's not about *her*. It's about *both* of you. A loving relationship will only work if both of you can fulfill one another's love and dedication. I have found out that we men are a little reluctant about that, because we are too prideful. We want to be the *alpha males* in the relationship. We want to run things without women having a say in any of our decisions. In this poem, I wanted to show everyone—especially women—that if they are in a relationship with me, I am going to give them all I have because of my love for them.

The letter of Paul in Ephesians 5 tells husbands to love their wives as much as they love themselves. I know I love myself.

I love what God has done with me, for me, and through me. Now you have to show your wife why you love the fact that God brought both of you together. You must love your wife the same way God loves the church. We need to throw away all our pride and arrogance and show the ladies that we are just as capable of being sensitive as they are. In doing so, our relationships will last longer, our unions will be stronger, and we all will have a better understanding of one another.

This poem is dedicated to the ladies who read the poem and thought, *This brother is soft!* It's not about being soft. It's about humbling ourselves as men of God—men of character and honor. It's about following the example that Christ led while He was on earth and the example that He continues to lead through others. There is definitely no shame in loving your wife as much as you love your own soul. Rather, there are rewards in this lifetime— and bigger rewards in heaven when you accept and allow Christ to be the central point in the relationship.

CHAPTER 27

Do You Take Her?

The Vow

Hearts race as you pace yourselves to the alter
Praying inside that your inner anxiety begins to falter
As you hold hands, you realize this is the moment of truth
You're the Adam to her Eve and the Boaz to her Ruth
You think back to the day that you were first engaged
that one time you and her were on the same page
The days when you shared countless laughs with her
When she was upset, you calmed her stormy weather
Side by side, you flew together, and here you stand
In front of family and friends, woman and man, hand in hand
A union of affection and love that God has sanctified
as groom and bride, for God to be glorified
Then you think about the future and what lies ahead
I have great faith in you based on the lives you led
Don't let the lies and the power of the devil deceive you
For I know that soon you'll have others who'll precede you
Two hearts beating together as one and the same
Two separate sparks that conjoin and ignite a flame
Two souls—refined, but not defined; intertwined, but not confined
Now as you take the vow for better, for worse, sickness, and health
You both may not be rich, but through God, you have abundant wealth
As you embark on a matrimonial quest filled with spiritual gain,
Know that your lives will never be the same.

Accepting the Vow

The day has finally arrived. It's a beautiful, sunny, spring day, and all around the chapel, white streamers and decorations cover the altar, the balcony, and the stage. Candles are lit, and the flowers seem to bloom as the guests begin to file in at the church to take their seats. The bridesmaids make last-minute preparations to their dresses and practice the formal walk down the aisle that they have been rehearsing for the past couple months. The flower girl stands by the door, waiting for her cue to step out and start spreading flowers in the aisle. Camera lights flash everywhere, capturing the beautiful scenery that surrounds the people.

The bride is in the dressing room, making sure her dress fits her absolutely perfectly. She does not want any mistakes during the wedding, as this is a day to be remembered. She gets a bit emotional, because she has been waiting for this day to come with both anticipation and anxiety. She looks in the mirror once again, and once everything is fine, she beckons one of the maids to tell the organ player to begin the bridal music.

In another room, the groom is also making sure that he is ready to take his bride's hand. He adjusts his necktie and fixes his tuxedo while his best man and some other close friends speak some words of confidence to him. The groom knows that he is about to make a decision—one of the biggest steps of his life. He is going to give up his bachelor lifestyle and trade it for a lifetime with his true love.

It all leads to this—the chance meeting, the dates, and the dinners. All the countless hours they both spent together will be concluded and justified upon this act of union. Now it is time. The groom and the best man take their places in front of the pastor performing the ceremony. The flower girl comes in; spreading flowers all around as the guests smile and reflect at her age and innocence. Then the bridesmaids follow right after, accompanied by the groom's friends and brothers. Finally, the moment that the groom has been waiting for arrives. The bride walks in alongside her father, who will perform the ceremonious rite of giving his daughter away.

The bride is as beautiful as the May weather outside. She stands next to her betrothed as the pastor reads the Bible to sanctify the union. The ring bearer walks in and gives the ring to the best man, who gives it to the groom. After the sanctification, the ring—which is a symbol of the endless love that they devoted to each other—is placed on the bride's finger, and in front of the people in the congregation, the groom and the bride kiss. It is a beautiful moment. Guests and family members are emotional, in a tearful state of joy. This is how marriage was designed to be—how it's meant to be.

Since the creation of man, God has given the example of marriage through the union of Adam and Eve to signify that two souls, once married, are one. The woman was originally created from the man's rib, so it only made sense that both members conjoin once more.

The ceremony of marriage has come a long way from the ancient days in the Bible. Back in the Bible days, there were certain rules regarding marriage and who was allowed to marry whom. For one thing, someone from one nation could not marry another nation. It was considered blasphemous and was very unsettling. The reasons foreign people did not intermarry were because of bloodlines, religion, and separation of races. Another mandatory aspect of marriage was that a person's marriage or partner had to be given by the parents. Parents ordained and arranged the marriage ceremonies. Any other way was not condoned at all. In some countries, marriage may still be that way, but one thing is certain—in universal marriage, there is a vow taken by groom and bride, confessing to man and to God absolute, unlimited love toward the other partner. That part doesn't change. No matter how it's done, marriage has the same meaning.

Marriage can be the result of divine intervention leading up to reunion. I will always cherish the story of Abraham's servant praying to God to provide Isaac with a wife. God plays more than a minor role in marriage—He plays a crucial role, because marriage comes with knowledge of your mate and agreement on certain things. The bride and the groom can disagree on many things, but they *must* agree on one thing. God has to be the focus of the marriage—the focus of the union. Too many marriages are done without the same sanctification in a hurried style, and marriages in which the partners do not take the time to reflect and thank the Lord for His part in the matchmaking of the couple will not last very long and will end up being broken very quickly.

This poem is dedicated not only to those who are already married, but to those who are thinking about taking that next step in their relationship. When the vow is taken between spouses, remember the example of the love Christ has for His church. Ephesians 5:31–32 states, "As the Scriptures say 'A man leaves his father and mother and is joined to his wife, and the two are united into one.' This is a great mystery, but it is an illustration of the way Christ and the church are one" (NLT).

PART 5

Last, but Definitely Not Least

"Whoever gives heed to instruction prospers and blessed is he who trusts in the Lord"

(Proverbs 16:20)(NIV).

CHAPTER 28

Feeling Trapped Inside

In the Belly of the Beast

You're frantically searching for a way out of the abyss,
With knowledge that nothing can be as dreadful as this
Our life's demons seem to strategize in a close huddle
as we struggle to swim out of our deep, muddy puddle
The adrenaline in our legs ignites us to sprint even more
but we remain rooted as if we're cemented to the floor
There's only so much pain and agony our bodies can take
As our demons infiltrate, then dehydrate us dry a flakes
The world's abandonment and isolation swallow us whole
even our poles of good works cannot rescue us from our holes
Starvation sets in now as our stomachs groan and protest
unless we put our heads together to escape our mess.
The beast seeks to destroy and hunt us down for its feast
it will attack us—from the loved ones to those loved the least
The beast represents the system that we live in today
As people created by God, we don't take the advice to watch and pray
Before we know it, we are already in the process of digestion,
Congestion, as our inner spiritual circle is experiencing infestation
Are you searching to escape the system and the industry?
You don't have to fear yourself or run away from me.
Believe the words that comes out of His mouth,
because believe it or not, there's a way out.

Being Digested by the System

"**B**ut the Lord provided a great fish to swallow Jonah, and Jonah was inside the fish three days and three nights. From inside the fish, Jonah prayed to the Lord his God. He said: 'In my distress I called to the Lord and he answered me. From the depths of the grave I called for help and you listened to my cry'"(Jonah 2:2) (NIV). Jonah finds himself in a situation no one wants to be in. Inside the dark, smelly stomach of a great fish (known in some versions to be a leviathan), Jonah had no else to turn to but God. The first thing Jonah did was acknowledge the Lord and thank Him for providing the fish to swallow him up so he would not perish in the sea. *What? Am I missing something?* Jonah was swallowed by a fish, and he thanked God for that? I didn't understand it at first, but slowly, I started to understand why Jonah was so grateful.

In the beginning of the book, Jonah was instructed by God to go to a country called Nineveh and preach against it. Due to the evil of that city, the Lord planned to destroy it. Jonah did not want to do it, and he tried running from God. He headed for Tarshish, now located in southern Spain. God saw him, and He caused a big storm to rock the boat Jonah was in. Jonah then understood that because he was on the boat, everyone else was suffering from the storm, too. Jonah then instructed the men aboard to throw him off of the boat so the storm would stop. The men did this, and the storm stopped. This made the sailors instant believers, and they offered sacrifices to God and made vows to Him.

Jonah, however, wasn't that lucky. The minute he hit the water, God sent a big fish to swallow him up. To this day, I still don't know how a man can be swallowed by a big fish and survive for three days in there, finally to be spit out onto dry land. It's near impossible. But we must remember that this is the God of the ages. *Impossible* is not even in His vocabulary.

Inspiration for this poem led me to believe that as humans, we are prideful and selfish. We don't realize that we live in a system that dictates our lifestyles. We dress in what people want or desire us to dress in. We go places that people want us to go, even when those places aren't healthy for us. The system teaches us to grow up, go to school, get a degree, get a good job, get married, have children, grow old, retire, and die. The system does not teach us to be different. The system does not teach us to be spiritually unique so that we can alter the way people live. Then whenever we mess up or make mistakes, the system is quick to judge us according to our actions. We are consumed by embarrassment and guilt, because we do not want to anger and upset the people running the system. It's like we're trapped in an ant farm and there are larger beings staring at us, watching our hard work, and making observations on us. It seems unjust—and that really is the way life is. The worst thing we can do is try to take matters into our own hands and make a bigger mess of things.

Instead of listening to God and daring to be different, Jonah chose to run from wisdom straight into the arms (or rather, the fins) of the system. Jonah ran from God—but he ran directly into trouble on his own. Taking our own path and our own way unconsciously is not going to lead us in the right direction. We always like to believe that we are in charge of our own lives. We are in charge of the *choices* we make in our lives. If we make the wrong choice, like Jonah did, and choose to be swallowed up by the system and the world, God—while a merciful God—is also a just God, and He will find a way to open our eyes or allow reality to set in. The only way to fight the system is with encouragement given by those close to us.

Good works are not going to be enough to escape the system. Sure, it's an outlet, because we all must work and do what we can to help others, but we can't help others until we help ourselves. The first thing we can do to help ourselves is to admit that we need help. The world is not going to take care of you. The streets are not going to take care of you.

I remember serving jury duty in 2008. The members of the jury took a trip to the county jail. I was taken aback by the number of inmates I saw. There were so many inmates that the facility was getting overcrowded. I couldn't help but feel sorry for the guys locked up. Their freedom was taken away from them. They lived their whole lives in the system, and they ended up on the wrong side of the system. They depended on the system—they ate, drank, and slept the system—and disobedience, pride, and following their own path put them in captivity. But let's remember that Jesus can overpower any system that we are living in. Jonah was in the belly of the fish for three days. Jesus died on the cross, and He rose on the third day. He was able to escape the belly of the beast. If you put your trust and faith in Him, He can help you escape, too. You will begin to see life from a whole other perspective.

CHAPTER 29

He's the Reason for the Season

Sign of the Star

Red and green illuminate the scene, making everything serene
Time stands still, as if we are living in our own subconscious dreams
Snow seems to cover the tops of every house, roof, and car,
But throughout all the excitement, we forget the sign of the star
Though it remains very far, the light burns bright from within,
no matter who we are, what we do, or where we've been
Stockings with small gifts hang over every doorway and fireplace,
there is a look of love and enjoyment on each and every face
You can taste the holiday meals as the smell lingers around,
reducing huge, urban, industrial cities into one Yule town.
Candy, ornaments, and holiday cheer engulf the pine tree
But the only image that captivates me is the nativity.
The defining moment in history, depicting the holy baby
known as the Prince of Peace—the true sign of a king
He is the reason why the choirs sing and the bells ring
He is the reason why those shepherds left their flocks,
He is the reason why we stare at the hands of the clock
waiting anxiously for the twenty-fifth to come at midnight's stroke
The King who broke all chains and barriers to relieve me of my yoke
The sign of the star saved me before I even knew myself,
and gave me a gift more valuable than St. Nick and his elf
He gave me the gift of life and the gift of free choice,
gave me the chance to praise Him with one sound—one voice
The Lamb who sacrificed Himself, enduring every cut and scar
Celebrate not only Christmas, but the sign of the star.

Christmastime Is Here

It's that time of year again. Sweet, old-time carols fill the nighttime air. Everyone seems to be in a happier mood, regardless of the situation that they're in. Department stores pitch sales everywhere, especially on outlets, toys, clothing, and food. Everywhere you look, green wreaths hang on doors. Carolers from the church are stopping by doors to sing joy into the hearts of people. I love this moment. I love Christmas.

Every year, when Christmas came, I anticipated the Christmas dinner. My mother would cook her delicious holiday ham, and my uncles, aunts, and cousins would come over and exchange gifts on Christmas Eve. The best movies are also shown around Christmas time. My brothers I and would had a tradition of watching twenty-four hours of *A Christmas Story*. I can still hear Flick's cry of desperation to his friends after getting his tongue stuck on the pole from a bet: "Come on, guys! Don't leave me here!" That part still gets me rolling.

I also loved watching the *Home Alone* movies—the ones starring McCauley Culkin. I loved *Home Alone* and *Home Alone 2*. *Home Alone 3* was all right, and even if the kid who replaced Culkin wasn't as smart as his predecessor, I still had to give him his props, because he handled *four* criminals! *Home Alone 4* was a complete bust. I wish they never released that film. That film was nowhere near as funny as the original two, and the criminals from that movie weren't even smart. The two inept criminals McCauley had to contend with, Marv and Harry, were actually smart guys who ran into a smarter kid. The best part in the whole movie was when Kevin McCallister (played by Culkin) was defending his home against the wet bandits, Marv and Harry. Kevin had *murdered* them with booby traps until Marv caught Kevin's foot when Kevin tried to escape. Kevin was in trouble. He had to do something. He saw his older brother's pet tarantula, and he grabbed it and planted it right on Marv's nose. Marv screamed like a baby, and the tarantula fell on Harry's chest. Marv then told Harry not to move. He grabbed a crowbar in hopes of killing the spider. He missed and accidentally hit Harry in the gut. Even now, I laugh myself into a frenzy at that part. They just don't make holiday movies like those anymore.

I'm not trying to make movies the focal point of this chapter, but there were a couple defining parts in *Home Alone*. One was when Kevin ran away from Harry and Marv. In fear, he ran into the closest, safest place to hide—a statue of the nativity. In another scene, Kevin came to the church, and he made amends with old man Marley, who was Kevin's neighbor and was rumored to have killed a man with a snow shovel. To me, the defining moment was that throughout the insane comedy in the movie, the picture did not steal glory away from the *true* meaning of Christmas. The nativity scene, the choir singing "O Holy Night," and the church where Kevin talked to old man Marley were subtle signs that reminded people the real reason we celebrate Christmas.

This is the reason for the season. God—through the Holy Spirit—allowed a virgin named Mary to give birth to Jesus, who would be the Savior of the world and whose kingdom would never end. His birth was the turning point in history and is one of the most celebrated events to this day. At the first Christmas, there were no Christmas decorations. There were no stockings, no chimneys for Santa, no Christmas trees with fancy wrapped gifts waiting to be torn to shreds by eager boys and girls around the world, and no Christmas lights. In fact, the only light that was around at the time was the light of the star that shone directly over the small inn at Bethlehem where Jesus was born.

The same light that gave the wise men direction to locate the King of kings in His humble abode was the light that shone within my heart the day I wrote this piece. The birth of Christ wasn't a huge fanfare. He was born in a tiny, rented stable where the animals were, because there was no room at any inn in Bethlehem. Most kings and men of royalty were born surrounded by greatness, riches, and power, but the Son of God did not come into the world with those things at His disposal. His birth was a simple birth, showing us that Jesus was a King—not only for the rich people, but for everybody who believed in Him. Every year, as I look at the star that hangs on the top of our Christmas tree, I think of it as the star that led to the salvation of man. I think of it as the star that led us right to Immanuel, which means "God is with us." I think of it as a point of navigation that I was blessed to have found. It has led me right to Christ. I also think about those who have seen the star but have not followed it and instead get lost looking for a way back into His glory. There are those who haven't even seen the star yet, and all they need to do is stop looking down, because there is nothing on the ground that can help them. If they looked up toward heaven, they would see the sign of salvation. It would lead them to the right place in their lives.

To some extent, Christmas has been stretched and labeled as a corporate American holiday because of the norm of buying gifts, getting the right Christmas tree, and preparing the dinner. Businesses are making more and more money with all the purchases people make. This is just my opinion, but Christmas should eventually lead you back to one place—the church. What better place is there to celebrate the birth of Christ than on the rock that God has built and called His church? Christmas time is not meant to be spent partying, going crazy, hanging mistletoe over doors, and trying to kiss one another. That's not what it's all about.

The best memories I had of Christmas were the times spent with my church family in Bethany Baptist Church in Queens, New York; First Haitian Baptist Church of Jonesboro; and Eastwood Baptist Church in Marietta, Georgia. Each place had its own special memory. Bethany had great Christmas specials and services where the kid's choirs would sing and act in drama performances. My first two acting roles in Christmas programs were at Bethany. As I grew up, I started to help the members prepare for Christmas, carrying the big tree up to the stage and decorating the church. The times I had with my friends were priceless. At Eastwood Baptist Church, we would do mission work on Christmas, going to nursing homes and singing carols for the elderly. We would also go door-to-door and sing carols for the people living in the Marietta area. In Jonesboro, I had the pleasure of writing a play for our youth in 2006 called *The True Meaning of Christmas*. It was the first skit I'd written, and when it was performed, it looked even better. The youth had fun rehearsing for it, and I had a good time writing it and assigning characters. Christmas time was the only time I remembered acting in a church play as a child in Bethany or writing and directing a play in Jonesboro.

Christmas has shown me how much I've grown from a follower to a leader, and I wouldn't trade those memories for anything in the world. The next time Christmas comes around, make some memories of your own. Honor God by going to church, and reflect on what He has done for you that year and how His coming down to earth has influenced you as a person. Take the time to thank God for placing His star in the sky to point us in the direction of Jesus Christ.

CHAPTER 30

He Comes to the Rescue

Hero

You've been there for me as long as I can remember,
From warm days in July to cold nights in December
You've been there for more than a century,
There are no words describing what You mean to me.
You've never required a long cape to fly around
or creep without a sound throughout the entire town
Your weapons are the elements that surround You
Your promises are the words that we cling to
The fight for what's right is Your main focus and drive
You breathe with a vibe that's loud and alive
You were born to be a leader upon conception;
to be a reflection of goodness without deception
Deep in your eyes; a dark past reveals its history
The reason You serve without reward's a mystery
You constantly appear and disappear in a quick flash
as You dash off to clash with the criminal's trash
Then as You complete Your battle with the greedy
You turn to the hungry, the poor, and the needy
As a child stares up at You with wistful eyes
He'll never forget Your road to ultimate self-sacrifice
He's still young and naive now, so he won't know why
But he'll always direct his eyes to the sky
Then he'll know why the sun shines—why the winds blow
He'll know by then that You were his hero.

Being a Hero

When you were a kid, people always asked you to write who the hero was in your life. You then took the time to reflect on who had been a hero to you. Some kids put famous actors, actresses, or athletes, and some even put their parents. As for me, the last time I was asked who my hero was, I wrote, "My hero is my dad, because he came from a country that did not have much, and he made it through this life and raised me in it."

My dad really was a hero to me, but I overlooked the greater hero behind him—Jesus Christ. My father did tell me that if it wasn't for Jesus Christ saving him when he was younger, he wouldn't be where he is today. As kids growing up in rough times, we needed a hero to look up to. Once again, the media portrays fictional heroes who swoop down to rescue us in the nick of time. When I was growing up, my favorite fictional heroes were Captain Planet, the Teenage Mutant Ninja Turtles, Batman, Superman, and Spider-man. I was hooked on those shows when I was younger. It was nice to visualize heroes coming down to save the world.

When I was eight or nine, I started drawing comics called "The Adventures of Super Marc." I know it may sound ridiculous, but I drew newspaper-like comics of myself in a cape and a *v* on my head for victory. I drew myself going against the vilest of villains (most of them were named after adults I didn't like!). It's funny, now that I think about it. The worst thing is that I don't have any copies of my drawings. I was not a good artist, but the comics had funny dialogue and great action. The characters started out as plain stick figures, and then they evolved to figures that were more filled out. When I was done, I played out the comics in my head. I got the idea from the Nickelodeon show *Doug,* in which the title character imagined himself as Quailman, a hero with a belt on his head and underwear outside his pants. He had a giant *Q* on his chest.

The comic phase lasted for a short time, simply because I got bored by comics. I grew up and understood reality a little bit more. I could spend my whole life trying to save the world, but the world will always be corrupt, and evil will always overrun it. Even if Batman, Superman, or any of the other characters were real, they couldn't be heroes forever. Men age and die, but the Word never dies. God sent the Word (Jesus) into the world for us to believe Him and know that our troubles on earth are only temporary. Let's be patient and wait on our real Hero.

CHAPTER 31

The Celestial City

Heaven

I can take you to a place with unlimited space
Where we can greet and integrate face-to-face
A place that we can call our own without interruption
Without wars, poverty, famine, or political corruption
A place where the grass is greener the sky's more blue
A spot that to you is too good to be true.
No more cancer, no more disease, and no dying
No more upsets, no more heartbreak, and no crying
A place where happiness and abundance are endless
For anyone who feels weak and defenseless.
A place where people dwell together in unity
One blameless, stainless, violence-free community
There are no guns, whips, chains, or knives
No drugs or wars with people losing their lives
There'll be no cars, no buses, and no trains
We'll all fly like eagles, so there'll be no planes
A place that is made of jasper, onyx, and gold
A place for the young and the old, the humble and bold
The temperature is mild, and it never gets cold.
A unique domain that is not present on Earth,
Its residence requires dedication and second rebirth.
Like a hotel, it does have a way of reservation
Once your name's been checked, you're in eternal vacation
You'll be treated as a prized guest.
Where service and quality are at their best;
Far more elegant and superior than all the rest.
Take my hand, and I'll guide you in
'Cause I know the Master within.

It's More than Just Clouds

More than once, I lay in my bed, wondering what it would be like when it was all over. I heard all the time that when we got there, everything would change—not just change, but change for the better. My only perception of heaven for the longest time was people dressed in all white on top of some clouds with little halos on our heads. *(Hmm*—maybe I watched *too* much television back then!) Cartoons showing WB characters portrayed twisted versions of heaven. The idea that when cartoon characters died, they went to heaven without any doubt did nothing to answer my question. What exactly was heaven? What would we do when we got there? Would going to Heaven end all our pain on earth? Or was it something that people love to express to make light of their situations?

All my questions were eventually answered, but I still can't help but think about what it'll be like. The first thing that we have to understand is that heaven is much more than a bunch of clouds with a golden gate hovering above the earth. Heaven is *not* of this earth. Heaven is where God resides—the Kingdom of the Lamb of God. As Jesus told Pilate in John 18:36 when he awaited crucifixion, "My kingdom is not of this world. If it were, my servants would fight to prevent my arrest by the Jews. But now my Kingdom is from another place" (NIV).

Jesus Himself said that His kingdom was not on earth. If it was meant to be, He could have called His servants to prevent His arrest by the Jews. By *servants,* He was not referring to His disciples or earthly followers. Jesus was referring to His heavenly hosts that serve Him. Jesus could have easily called a legion of angels to save Him from dying and wage war with His enemies, but He chose to fulfill the prophecy set by the prophet Isaiah years before. I thank God that He did not send down the army of angels to attack, because there was no way human soldiers could fight against angels of God. Remember the two guards watching the tomb of Jesus until the day He rose again? They saw only *one* angel, and they fainted and became "like dead men."(Matthew 28:3)(NIV) Imagine seeing an army of angels with weapons coming right at you! They would definitely change the world as we know it today.

In the kingdom of heaven, where will we be? In John 14, Jesus explains that in His Father's house, there are many rooms. The best thing about it is that there is no more fighting for space with annoying siblings! There is room for everybody who gets in. Jesus also said that He has prepared a place for us and that He will come back to take us with Him so we can be with Him forever. He ends by saying, "You know the way to the place where I am going"(John 14:4) (NIV). If we are truly saved—*biblically saved*—we know the way to heaven. *Jesus* is the way to heaven. There is no other way to heaven or to God but Jesus. Some people have a hard time accepting this, but it is the truth.

Jesus is also the *truth.* In John 14:6, Jesus says, "I am the Way, the Truth, and the Life. No one comes to the Father but through me" (NIV). Jesus is the way to heaven. He epitomizes truth in every way and form, and in Him, there is life. That's why in the poem, I mentioned that just like a hotel, heaven does require a reservation. When you check in to a hotel, you arrange, you pay your dues, and when you've done all you can at your end, your name is on the reservation. It's the same way with us in our spiritual lives. What have we done to fulfill or enhance our spiritual walk with Christ? What have we done to invite others to make that same spiritual reservation? We eat to nourish our bodies; the nutrients dissolve and evolve into usable energy for our bodies. Do we take the Word of God into the same consideration? To set up a reservation for heaven, we must first *reserve* and *preserve* the teachings and the values of the Lord in our hearts.

When we get to heaven's gate, our entrance is going to be determined by our name's appearance in the Book of Life. I know that when it's all been said and done, all I want to hear from God is that I've done well in serving Him, I've done my best to show my desire to be used by Him, and my ticket's punched for heaven.

Another description of heaven is the pure beauty of the place itself. Heaven also represents the New Jerusalem that will be part of the new heaven and new earth. The streets are made of gold, and they are as pure as glass. Foundations of the city are built with jasper, sapphire, chalcedony, emerald, sardonyx, carnelian, beryl, and other gems I don't know! I'm already excited, because it'll be something unexpected and new. But nothing that is impure will ever enter it, nor will anyone who does what is shameful or deceitful, but only those written in the Lamb's book of Life. I call it the Celestial City, as in John Bunyun's book *The Pilgrim's Progress,* which talks about a Christian's tough road to heaven. It's hard, but it's rewarding in the end when our burdens are lifted and we can let the pain of this world drop from our shoulders.

CHAPTER 32

Are You Lost?

Where We At?

Driving down life's highways, gateways, and freeways,
The cycle spins and swerves as we waste our weekdays
We have weak days, but we take it as just another phase
We don't take it with grace, and we rush into a blaze,
Life as we know it will not slow down and wait
In this time and date, we should relax and relate

The roads are aligned with the same identical malign
Concealed so it could trip us and leave us behind
Our eyes don't see what we seem to perceive
We act happy and relieved, when in truth, we grieve
The enemy clouds judgment; we are intoxicated with hate
The ride veers to the side, help appears to be late

As though we were cursed, we take a spin for the worst
Sliding beyond our checkpoint, we remember the verse
"He will never leave you nor forsake you"
Some way, somehow, we persevere; we make it through
When our world's closing in and we feel lost, isolated, and trapped
Only He knows where you at; He holds the future's map.

What's Holding Us Back?

Some of us drive quite a distance to go somewhere and have to be there at a certain time. Don't you hate it when there are roadblocks constantly in your way? You're on your way to work, and you're about to be late. You make your best effort to leave the house as early as possible, and you count on the day going by smoothly for you. The minute your car takes the road, a number of bad things happen. You get stuck in midday traffic, and you're moving at a speed of about 2 mph. The worst thing is that when the traffic seems to subside, the driver straight ahead of you doesn't want to hurry up. Or imagine you're driving along the road, and suddenly, the front side of your car seems to tilt over. Frustrated, you step out of the car and examine the damage. Your tire is stuck in a pothole. What makes matters worse is that there is a construction nail stuck on the tire. Your tire will lose air in a couple weeks if you don't do something quickly—but that's the least of your worries. Throughout all these issues, you ask yourself, "Where am I? What am I even doing here? How did I get myself in this situation?"

Life is a long, tough road, and though we are the drivers, we experience obstacles along the way. But we have a goal that we are driving towards, and that is something all of us have in common. We strive to get ourselves to the next level in life.

For example, if you are studying in a medical field, you know the path to becoming a doctor is not going to be easy. Aside from being in school, for about three or four years after college, you have to earn your doctorate—you have to deal with the reality of operations, surgical tools, and witness the beginning and the end of life. The devil uses false inspiration to divert us from achieving our true goals. We want to be better people, but we have to start somewhere. We need a GPS—a navigator to guide us through this life. When our time comes, we will reach our ultimate goal—eternity. The last thing we need to do is close our eyes to our troubles and act as if nothing is wrong. We need to open our eyes to the true direction of God, using His ways. Psalm 119:105 says, "Thy word is a lamp unto my feet and a light unto my path" (KJV). Use Him to guide your path, and then you'll know where you truly are.

CHAPTER 33

In Memory of Virginia Tech Victims

Good-bye (In Memory of the Virginia Tech Shooting Victims)

Some people were in class, and some people were still sleeping
They had no idea that in a few hours, their parents would be weeping
Some people had parties the night before;
they came to their dorms at four
Some people probably had tests to study for.
Girls were swimming in their closets, looking for clothes
They didn't know when they stared in the mirror, it was their last pose
Guys were discussing their futures over bottles of wine or beer
They had no clue that tomorrow, they won't have a career
One dorm house continued to work through the day
They didn't know there was a killer bent on making them pay
One by one, students begin to enter classroom doors
They had no idea their blood would dampen the floor

Some people were going to grow up to be educators and teachers,
Perhaps a few of them were going to be preachers
Some people were going to be electricians or technicians
Some people were striving to be powerful politicians
Girls made plans for their marriages and motherhood
They saw the future ahead of them, and it looked really good
Instead, they are physically dead, entering eternally
People who were professors, students, and brothers in fraternities
Where they end up—that's up to Jesus Christ, our Lord
But we must face the fact that they are no longer here anymore
So I hope that one day, I will see them in heaven when I die
Then it won't ever have to be good-bye.

In Memory of Virginia Tech Victims

Imagine sitting in a classroom on a routine weekday, trying to stay awake so you can listen to the material that your teacher is trying to teach you. Your eyelids start to droop, and you soon begin to feel really drowsy. Deep inside, you think, *Why do I need to learn this stuff?* The guy in front of you is already sleeping, and by the looks of it, he's in pretty deep. It's a nice spring day. You stare out at the window, wishing that the day was more eventful. It is just *too* boring. You hope something happens.

Then without warning, you get what you wanted—but not in the way that you expected. A crazed man comes into the classroom, brandishing a gun. Classmates scream in terror and run for cover. Frantically, you try to find a desk to duck under for cover. In horror, you watch as your classmates, one by one, get shot and fall in pools of their own blood. You can't get the screams out of your head. That noise will stay inside of you for the rest of your life. You hear a giant *thud* as you see one of your friends fall to the ground, eyes wide open in a stare of shock as blood is pouring from the bullet wound in his head. Fighting back tears, you gaze toward the front door. It's ajar, so if you time it just right, you can sneak out the back and run for help as fast as you can.

Gathering the little strength that you have left, you use your instincts to find your way to the door. You try to open the handle.

Click. That's all you hear—but it isn't the click of the door. It is the click of a gun barrel pointed directly behind your head. Drenched in sweat, you turn around to look at the killer and realize that he looks familiar. As a matter of fact, you *know* this guy. He is not the most athletic person; he's extremely clumsy and lanky. You remember laughing with your friends when they joked about him. You plead for your life. "Please let me go. I promise I won't mess with you anymore."

The murderer stares at you with a mixture of hatred and indifference. You realize that you will not make it out the door to call for help. You won't make it back to your family for the holidays. You won't finish school or get your degree. You won't be able to grow up and be successful. The murderer knows he has your heart and your fate in his hands. He gets excited just knowing this, and her raises the gun, checking the rounds to make sure his bullets are accounted for. You close your eyes, hoping that it will be over quickly. The man pulls the trigger. No, you aren't dreaming, this is really happening. You hear two sharp shots before you feel it. He looks down at your body while you slump to the ground. You stare at your own blood as it flows from your body to the ground. You remember how you always wanted to live your life and how you were going to make sure you lived to experience life growing up. It doesn't look like that's going to happen. The gunman raises his gun to finish the job he has started with you. You wanted some action; well now you've got what you asked for.

On Monday, April 16, 2007 a man known as Cho Seung-Hui, a senior at Virginia Tech, committed one of the most massive murders in American history, killing thirty-three people, including himself. Many people did not wake up that morning thinking they were going to die in the next couple hours. As a college student myself, I couldn't help but feel different waves of emotion all at once. I felt a wave of anger toward Cho and a wave of remorse for the victims' families, who were going through a lot at that moment. I couldn't quite place the reason a man would kill so many people all at once without further question. I wrote this piece as a legacy to the victims. I wanted to show that I too grieved for that loss.

The Dedicated Reading

It was the month of May, about three or four weeks after the shooting at Virginia Tech occurred. The First Haitian Baptist Church of Jonesboro had been invited to a talent show held at Open Bible Haitian Church in Marietta, Georgia. There were Haitian churches from everywhere—Orlando, Georgia, Tennessee, South Carolina, New Jersey, New York, and Washington, DC. The talent show included a choir competition, poetry reading, solo singing, dancing, etc. The pastor of Jonesboro wanted me to write a poem as an entry into the talent show, and I spent about a week figuring out what I was going to write. Then I felt God speaking to me, telling me to write a poem dedicated to the victims at Virginia Tech.

On the day of the talent show, at the last minute, I wrote this poem as I reflected on the thirty-three people who lost their lives. Then we were on our way to the talent show. The talent displayed was outstanding. Finally, my name was called. Nervously, I walked onstage, with about a million eyes on me. Slowly and calmly, I read the poem, raising the suspense with every sentence I read. There were other poetry entries, and they were good, but mine was better. When I finished reading it, the whole place exploded with claps and cheers. I remember feeling really good about myself—but most of all, I felt like I paid my respect to the Virginia Tech victims that day.

The time for the awards came. For each section, the judges gave a third-, second-, and first-place trophy. In the poetry reading contest, Open Bible Church came in third. Then another church came in second. We held our breaths and waited on who won the first place award. Then I heard Jonesboro's name called out loud for the first place. Our small group of members got up and celebrated as I took the trophy for first place. I gave the trophy to the church so the members could always remember what I did that day.

I won the trophy for the poem and the way I read it, but I really didn't do it for the prize. I wanted my culture to understand the seriousness of the alienation that leads up to school violence. I wanted people to learn that if we don't reach out to others in their time of need or if we isolate ourselves from them, it may lead them to harm themselves and others. The greatest commandment Jesus gave us was to love Him with all our heart, soul, strength, and mind. The second commandment was to love our neighbors as ourselves. If we take those commandments and lessons to heart, God will put us on a much higher level than we are right now. Before I read that poem at the talent show, I didn't really read my poems anywhere else except for Eastwood Baptist and Jonesboro. I still lacked the courage and confidence in myself to read my poem in front of strangers. However, on that day, my fear barrier broke, and I became more assertive and confident in my gift. I was no longer unsure and asking questions.

Although the shooting at Virginia Tech was a great tragedy, God used that to instill confidence in me. God used that piece to break my barrier—so in a way, I'm thankful that He used me for that purpose. Those who perished on that fateful day did not die in vain. Their untimely end has made me spiritually and intellectually strong, and I do hope that if they were saved, I get to see some of them in heaven.

CHAPTER 34

Am I Losing It?

Nightmares

I dreamt that I was in a desolate, deserted land hit hard by drought
The inhabitants lost all sense of decorum and
dignity as inner beasts came out
Wild and primitive, with their teeth, they
tugged and tore the flesh of nature,
eating every living animal, those with feathers and those with fur
It never occurred to me that they lived that way until they saw me today,
Buildings were falling down—the places
that were once colorful were gray
Animalistic and cannibalistic were those people I was surrounded by,
compounded by and grounded by, while I could do nothing but stand by
It was then that I realized I was the only human being surviving,
yet I felt like I was dying in darkness so strong that it was blinding
My vision was that of death as all goodness was laid to rest,
I noticed the looks of detest etched on the intellectually less
With long, dirty hands unkempt, they attempted to drag me to their hell
Then behind me, a ravine opened up, and I begin falling and as I fell,
.....my hair was standing up in a rush of reaction and adrenaline
as a cold breeze blew from outside, penetrating me with frigid wind
Cold sweat blanketed my face as I strove to erase what I just saw
The dark, deep vision of hell and strange beings eating animals raw.

A Glimpse Into a Life Without Christ

Is it possible that some dreams can predict the future? It's very possible, based on biblical evidence. In the book of Genesis, Pharaoh had a dream predicting seven years of plenty and seven years of drought in Egypt. God used Joseph to interpret the dream and save the land. The prophet Daniel also interpreted a dream that King Nebuchadnezzar had.

There are times during which dreams had an impact on the words that were written, but I never had a dream that was as vivid and real as the one that inspired this piece. In my dream, I looked around, and the first thing that I noticed was the *darkness* that I was surrounded by. There was no sun or moon; the only light that was available was from a few broken streetlights. I walked around and noticed empty, abandoned houses. There were no street signs. Suddenly, I saw a figure dart beside me. The movement was so quick, I didn't know if it was a man or a beast. For just one split second, I looked down, and chills ran down my spine. The street that I was walking on was full of dead, half-eaten animals. It was the most grotesque scene I've ever witnessed. Bodies of squirrels, birds, rabbits, and other forest creatures littered the ground. One of the abandoned houses had dead animals hanging from what seemed to be a clothesline.

I want to take this time to excuse myself for the disturbing descriptions and images that I may place in somebody's thoughts. I feel that by explaining the dream that I had at the time, it could open your eyes to what the world can be like. In a flash, I saw someone again—a human being. *Whew.* I sighed and thought all the danger had passed. But when I took a closer look at the person, they had sharp teeth and long nails. They were monstrous, deadly individuals. I remember running for my life. I heard footsteps, indicating that they were pursuing me. I couldn't hide my fear. With a jolt, I realized that I was the only man on earth. I know this sounds like a plot from the movie *I Am Legend,* but it felt true. It looked true. It even *smelled* true. I ran into one of the abandoned houses, thinking I got away. But as soon as I flipped on a light switch, I saw that somehow the creatures were in the house. They grabbed at me with their long fingers and long, brownish nails. They pressed in with their malnourished bodies. I was going to be next on their menu; there was no escaping it ... then I woke up. I've had nightmares before, and I usually shrugged them off, but this one was different. I couldn't shake it off, and I thought about the last days and what the world would be like leading up to Judgment Day.

It's also possible that I was looking at an alternate reality in which God did *not* send His Son to die on the cross. Instead of sending down His gift, He withheld it from us, because we were living in evil. It was just like *Back To the Future, Part 2,* in which Marty McFly stole a sports almanac from the future in hopes of becoming a millionaire. He tried to bring the book back to his time so he could predict the outcome of every sporting event. However, when a bully from Marty's past got his hands on the almanac, the bully went back to *his* time and used the book to make an alternate reality where the world was mean, corrupt, and crime reigned everywhere.

When I woke up from my dream, I sat for about fifteen minutes, shocked by how real and vivid the dream was. Then I felt a rush of gratitude toward God that He did not leave us in that type of world (if it was, in fact, an alternate reality without Christ). One thing I remembered from reading *Robin Hood* was what Robin Hood's sidekick, Little John, said after Robin had a dream that he was beaten up and left for dead at the side of the road. He said, "Don't worry about dreams, master. They are of no more weight than the wind." Little John was stating that we cannot let a dream dictate the way we live our lives. The dream I had may have been a false image planted in my head by the deceiver to shake my faith and live in fear of the future.

How can we discern messages sent by God from the messages that are not from God? The answer is probably the setting. Where God resides, there is light. There is happiness and there are no problems, sickness, death, or sin. Where the devil resides, there is evil, weeping, gnashing of teeth, and an eternity of misery. When I attempt to witness the gospel of Christ to people and I tell them that based on their lives, without Christ, they would be guilty in the eyes of God and would go to hell, I can't stand it when their reply is, "We are already living in hell." I think, *You have no idea.* If people think that this is bad, it's only going to get worse unless they open their eyes to the truth and soften their hearts. If we change our lives for the better, we don't have to experience that future or worry about living without our Savior. Once again, it's a choice. God gives us free will, and He doesn't force us to accept Him. But He would love for us to live within Him as He lives within us.

CHAPTER 35

Behold the Lamb

Look Upon Me

Your feet are worn out. You've been hungry; you've been weak
the future is so bleak that you don't think you can last another week
You have no one else to turn to for comfort and safety,
Then wherever you look, fresh perils call for more security
You've been torn, battered, beaten, and severely bruised
Everywhere you look, little children are getting harassed and abused
Women are being used, and the human race is dazed and confused
Your country's been split in two; no one can see you through
On your knees, you cry and you beg, "What must I do?"
Look into My eyes, and you'll see My care and My concern
Because I want you to learn that there's no reason to mourn
Look upon My hands, because with them, I have built hope
Where you can cope in a future without alcohol abuse or dope
You will be healed from any sickness; just witness from within
All you have to do is open your heart and soul and let Me in
Look upon My body and see that I've taken your beating,
afflicted and bleeding; My love is still proceeding while sin is receding
Sin's bite is deadly, but hell is worse if you ain't ready,
Be rid of all your guilt; turn to the cross, and look upon Me
It's for you that I'm hanging on this old, rugged tree,
Look upon Me, and you'll see and feel My mercy
Don't shun or curse Me; rather, thirst for Me,
because you are the first in Me.

Look Him Up

Perhaps the most important chapter in the inspiration of this poem comes directly from the Word of God, which tells us to look upon Him throughout all situations. I did a Bible study on Numbers 21:4–9. In this passage, Moses led the people of Israel around the land of Edom. The people began to complain and murmur against Moses and against God. This wasn't anything new, because anytime the road got worse and famine overtook the land, God's people always groaned and complained—mostly because of physical discomfort. God was fed up with the grumbling of the people, and He sent poisonous snakes among the people. These lethal creatures bit as many people as possible, injuring some and killing many. Try to picture that scene. Remember the motion picture *Snakes on a Plane*? In the movie, a wanted murderer filled the plane's cargo with poisonous snakes to kill the only witness on board who could lock him away. As soon as the plane was airborne, the cages that held the snakes opened, and the snakes escaped the cargo and slithered through vents and baggage holds and attacked the helpless passengers. It made for a very gory movie scene. (I wouldn't recommend it for children!)

The people of Israel were helpless, and they slowly died from the venom that constricted their bloodstreams. In desperation, they pleaded to Moses to pray to God to take away the snakes.

Moses heeded the pleas and earnestly turned to God on behalf of the suffering people. God told Moses to build a replica of a snake out of bronze on a pole and erect it so that everyone could see it. This was done, and as soon as Moses erected the snake in the presence of the people, whoever had snake bites looked upon it, and they were healed instantly.

This passage illustrates the most basic of Christian values. Look upon Jesus Christ, and you will live. In a sense, the bronze snake in the desert represented Christ. Jesus even referred to himself as the bronze snake in the desert. In John 3:14–15, Jesus said, "Just as Moses lifted up the snake in the desert, so the Son of Man must be lifted up, that everyone who believes in him may have eternal life" (NIV). Jesus was betrayed by one of His disciples, arrested, beaten, and finally crucified on a cross in the presence of the Jews. Jesus was erected in front of the people, just as the bronze snake of God in the desert. A series of different events happened while Jesus was on the cross. The sky grew dark in the ninth hour, and then there was a tremendous earthquake. The temple and the veil were split in two, and they crumbled. When people witnessed this, they exclaimed, "Surely he was the Son of God!" They finally *believed* He was the son of God. After calling Him a blasphemer and a heretic (which indicates being crazy and saying crazy things), they were finally convinced that what this man was saying all along could be true. But it's not just a possibility; it is a fact.

Jesus Christ was—and still is—the Son of God. He died on Calvary for you and me. All He wants us to do is look upon Him and believe. It says that when Jesus returns to claim His church, every knee shall bow, and every tongue shall confess that He is Lord. So if we believe Him now, even though we cannot physically see Him, that shows a great testament of our faith in the unseen.

There was a song released in the late nineties by Stacie Orrico called "Don't Look at Me." I love that song. In the song, Stacie is trying to emphasize that the focal point shouldn't be her. Yes, she is a singer, and yes, she loves what she does, but in this song, she turns the attention away from her onto Jesus Christ.. If we want to know who Christ really is and want to reach that point at which serving Christ is not routine or an everyday thing but a privilege, we must look upon Him. We can't turn away from God and say that we still trust Him.

Did some people turn away from the snake when it was erected? It's possible, because there were some people who were skeptical of the power of God. Some were skeptical of the fact that looking at a snake could heal. Are there still people today who don't look up to Christ because they are skeptical? Are there people who don't believe that God can heal them in their time of need? Yes, there are definitely people who feel that way. But if you want healing, and if you want His power manifested around you, in you, and through you, there is no other way to look but up. Let's not allow pride, disbelief, anger, and trials to blind us, because those are the tools that the enemy uses the most against us.

God may not come at the time you desire, but He will come through in the nick of time. Stay patient and steadfast in your Christian walk, and the Word will pay off in the future when there is no more pain or strife. You will live and breathe new life for all eternity.

ABOUT THE AUTHOR

Marc Arthur Beausejour was born in Queens, New York, on July 28, 1987. He has been writing poetry since the age of twelve. His poems have been recited, read, and published in church and school newsletters throughout the years. In an era that has seen the rise of prominent Haitian-American poets, Marc is set to solidify himself as one of the best poets of his time. Marc moved from New York to Kennesaw, Georgia in 2001 with his family and graduated from North Cobb High School in 2005. He is currently twenty-three years of age, working on his BA in Communications. He is employed by Ryla Teleservices in Kennesaw, Georgia.

THIS ISN'T THE END

TWO BONUS POEMS FROM THE
UPCOMING SECOND BOOK

RISING HIGHER THAN EVER

Another Hand Reaches Out

She lies at the corner of the dirty alley, blood trickling down her chin,
No one knows where she's been, and all that she can see is *Him*.
He leers and sneers toward her,
reviving memories of her abusive childhood
A vision of her estranged father, who would beat her as hard as he could,
leaving her with emotional and physical scars
that she has concealed for years
Until new danger rears its grotesque, blackened
head, raising her worst fears
Once considered the belle of the ball,
she once felt that she could have it all,
A handsome, debonair, yet deceptive young
man would lead to her downfall.
He tells her she is beautiful beyond compare—
beyond the clothes that she wears
Slowly but subtly, he undresses her physically
and mentally until she stands bare,
He teaches her how to use her body to get
anything she wants in the world.
Now if she had the choice, she would trade every
dollar, dime, diamond, and pearl.
Feeling empty and withered like an,unquenched rose, vase out of place,
her mind swims with the images of different
men who she can still smell and taste.
The man she took to be charming and handsome
turned out to be cruel and insane,
a pimp who has gambled her for money and
fame without a penny to her name.
Time after time, he has beaten her into submission
without any remorse or remission.
She now lies battered and bruised from the hair
on her head to her legs and thigh,
The pain is so intense in the sense that all she can do is lie there and cry.
Let the stream of tears flow so that everybody
or nobody would hear or know,
Another hand reaches out and she cringes,
expecting another backhand blow.
But this hand is much more real, much more
genuine—so friendly, yet so unknown,
All that she knows, though, is that this hand also has scars of its own.

Bound No More

For the longest time, my guilt has been weighing heavily in my chest
But false visions of being the best did not allow me to confess.
All I saw was my own vanity, slowly driving me to insanity,
My mind plagued with the chains of sex, lust, and profanity.
But within me I kept hearing Your voice, beseeching me to return
Even though my sinful nature resumed to consume me in slow burn
You never gave up on me, even though I give up on You so many times
I continually cover my good potential behind my secret inner crimes
Enjoying the pleasures of sin for a season continues to look appealing
But I'm sick of the games that I'm playing; I'm sick of concealing;
the fact that I am nothing but a prisoner bound in my own mess
When all I can do is call unto You; and to You, I would leave the rest.
I leave all the hate and anger that I've been trying to suppress
I leave all my demon-possessed company at the palm of Your hand
The one who left all His heavenly glory to become an earthly man,
without blemish, without sin, without any type of worldly fault.
You pole-vault over ideology, modern philosophy, without any occult
At my worst, all-time low, You came from above to descend below
I didn't understand why You did so, but now I start to know.
You've knocked at my heart's door, and all I can do is worship and adore
Because of You, I am no longer lost, but I have been found
and I have been freed because the world no longer has me bound.
As though the bars were made out of dried sticks, I break out of my cell
Thanking the Lord Jesus Christ that I am not bound for hell.